SHAMBHALA POCKET LIBRARY

THE BOOK OF
FIVE RINGS

Miyamoto Musashi

TRANSLATED FROM THE JAPANESE BY
Thomas Cleary

INCLUDING
*The Book of Family Traditions
on the Art of War*

by *Yagyū Munenori*

SHAMBHALA · Boulder · 2018

3 9082 13655 4014

SHAMBHALA PUBLICATIONS, INC.
4720 Walnut Street
Boulder, Colorado 80301
www.shambhala.com

© 1993 by Thomas Cleary

9 8 7 6 5 4 3 2 1

Printed in the United States of America

∞ This edition is printed on acid-free paper that meets the
American National Standards Institute z39.48 Standard.
♻ This book is printed on 30% postconsumer recycled paper.
For more information please visit us at www.shambhala.com.

Shambhala Publications is distributed worldwide by Penguin
Random House, Inc., and its subsidiaries.

THE LIBRARY OF CONGRESS CATALOGUES THE PREVIOUS EDITION
OF THIS BOOK AS FOLLOWS:
Miyamoto, Musashi, 1584–1645.
[Gorin no sho. English]
The book of five rings /by Miyamoto Musashi; a new translation
from the Japanese by Thomas Cleary, including Family traditions
on the art of war, by Yagyū Munenori.—1st ed.
p. cm.—(Shambhala dragon editions)
Includes bibliographical references.
ISBN 9781570627484 (Shambhala Dragon Editions)
ISBN 9781611806403 (Shambhala Pocket Library)
1. Military art and science—Early works to 1800. 2. Swordplay—
Japan—Early works to 1800. I. Yagyū Munenori, 1571–1646.
Hyōhō kadensho. English. 1993. II. Title.
U101.M5913 1993 92-56443 CIP
355.5'47—dc20

CONTENTS

No Sword   153

TRANSLATOR'S PREFACE

The Japanese word *shin-ken* means "real sword," but it is now more generally used in a metaphorical sense. In common parlance, to do something with a real sword means to do it with utmost earnestness. To have an attitude proper to a real sword means to be deadly serious. *Shin-ken shō-bu*, literally a contest with real swords, means something done in deadly earnest.

This molecule of linguistic anthropology hints at a very good reason why the Japanese are as persistent and skilled as they are at survival and adaptation. Through centuries of cultural training under the martial rule of the samurai, the Japanese are generally able to experience and address virtually anything as a life and death situation.

This book shows how they do it.

TRANSLATOR'S
INTRODUCTION

The Book of Five Rings and *The Book of Family Traditions on the Art of War* are two of the most important texts on conflict and strategy emerging from the Japanese warrior culture. Originally written not only for men-at-arms, they are explicitly intended to symbolize processes of struggle and mastery in all concerns and walks of life.

The Book of Five Rings was written in 1643 by Miyamoto Musashi, undefeated dueler, masterless samurai, and independent teacher. *The Book of Family Traditions on the Art of War* was written in 1632 by Yagyū Munenori, victorious warrior, mentor of the Shōgun, and head of the Secret Service.

Both authors were professional men-at-arms born into a long tradition of martial culture that had ultimately come to dominate the entire body of Japanese polity and society. Their writings are relevant not only to members of the ruling military caste, but also to leaders in other professions, as well as people in search of individual mastery in whatever their chosen path.

The *Book of Five Rings* and *The Book of Family Traditions on the Art of War* are both written in Japanese, rather than the literary Chinese customary in elite bureaucratic, religious, and intellectual circles in Japan at that time. The Japanese in which they are written, furthermore, is relatively uncomplicated and quite free of the subtle complexities of classical high court Japanese. Although the crudity of Musashi's syntax and morphology make for clumsy reading, nevertheless the basic simplicity and deliberate clarity of both works make them accessible to a wide and varied audience.

The rise and empowerment of the samurai class in Japan may be seen in the two terms used to refer to its members, *samurai* and *bushi.* The word *samurai* comes from the Japanese verb *saburau,* which means "to serve as an attendant." The word *bushi* is Sino-Japanese and means "armed gentry." The word *samurai* was used by other social classes, while the warriors referred to themselves by the more dignified term *bushi.*

The original samurai were attendants of nobles. In time their functions expanded to the administration, policing, and defense of the vast estates of the nobles, who were mostly absentee landlords. Eventually the samurai demanded and won a greater share of the wealth and political power that the nobles had called their own. Ultimately the military paragovernment of the

Shōguns, known as the Bakufu, or Tent Government, overshadowed the imperial organization and dominated the whole country.

Musashi and Yagyū lived in the founding era of the third Tent Government, which lasted from the beginning of the seventeenth century through the middle of the nineteenth century. While inheriting the martial traditions of its predecessors, this third Tent Government differed notably in certain respects.

The first Tent Government was established in eastern Japan near the end of the twelfth century and lasted for nearly one hundred and fifty years. The warriors of this time were descendants of noble houses, many of whom had honed their martial skills for generations in warfare against the Ainu people in eastern Japan. As the Tent Government was seated in Kamakura, a small town near modern Tōkyō, this period of Japanese history is commonly called the Kamakura era.

The second Tent Government supplanted the first in 1338. The warrior class had expanded and become more differentiated by this time, with lesser and thinner genealogical ties to the ancient aristocracy. The Shōguns of this period established their Tent Government in Kyōto, the old imperial capital, and tried to establish high culture among the new samurai elite. This period of Japanese history is commonly called the Ashikaga era, after the surname of the Shōguns, or the

Muromachi era, after the name of the outlying district of Kyōto in which the Tent Government was located.

To understand Japanese history and culture, it is essential to realize that no government ever united the whole country until the Meiji Restoration of 1868. The imperial government had always ruled the whole land in theory, but never in fact. The imperial house had never really been more than a center of powerful factions, competing with other powerful factions. Even when everyone recognized the ritual and political status of the emperor in theory, direct imperial rule only reached a portion of the land.

As this is true of the imperial house, so it is also true of the military governments. The reign of the Shōguns was always complicated and mitigated by the very nature of the overall Japanese power structure. The rule of the Kamakura Tent Government was not absolute, that of the Muromachi Tent Government even less. Separatism, rivalry, and civil warfare marked the fifteenth and sixteenth centuries.

By this time, known as the era of the Warring States, the way of war was open to anyone who could obtain arms by any means. Lower-class samurai rose up to overthrow the upper-class samurai, and Japan was plunged into chaos. It was not until the latter part of the sixteenth century that a series of hegemons emerged with strategy and power sufficient to move dramatically toward unification. The third Tent Government was built on the achievements of those hegemons.

Within the context of traditional Japanese society, the founder of the third Shogunate was an upstart and a usurper. Aware of this, he set out to establish a most elaborate system of checks and controls to ensure the impossibility of such an event ever occurring again. Moving his capital again to eastern Japan, away from the heartland of the ancient aristocracy and imperial regime, the new Shōgun disarmed the peasants and disenfranchised the samurai class, removing all warriors from the land and settling them in castle towns. This period of Japanese history is commonly known as the Tokugawa era, after the surname of the Shōguns, or the Edo period, after the name of the new capital city, now called Tōkyō.

Tokugawa Japan was divided into more than two hundred baronies, which were classified according to their relationship to the Tokugawa clan. The barons were controlled by a number of methods, including regulation of marriage and successorship, movement of territories, and an elaborate hostage system. The baronies were obliged to minimize their contingents of warriors, resulting in a large number of unemployed samurai known as *rōnin,* or wanderers.

Many of the disenfranchised samurai became schoolteachers, physicians, or priests. Some continued to practice martial traditions, and to teach them to others. Some became hooligans and criminals, eventually to constitute one of the most serious social problems of the later Tokugawa period. Certain differences, both technical and philosophical, between *The Book of Five Rings* and *The Book of Family Traditions on the Art of War* stem from the fact that Miyamoto Musashi was a masterless samurai pursuing a career as a dueler and an independent teacher of martial arts, while Yagyū Munenori was a distinguished war veteran and a servant of the central military government.

THE BOOK OF FIVE RINGS

More properly titled in English *The Book of Five Spheres,* Miyamoto Musashi's work is devoted to the art of war as a purely pragmatic enterprise. Musashi decries empty showmanship and commercialization in martial arts, focusing attention on the psychology and physics of lethal assault and decisive victory as the essence of warfare. His scientifically aggressive, thoroughly ruthless approach to military science, while not universal among Japanese martialists, represents a highly concentrated characterization of one particular type of samurai warrior.

Although a vast body of legend grew up around his dramatic exploits, little is known for certain about the life of Miyamoto Musashi. What he says of himself in *The Book of Five Rings* is the primary source of historical information. He killed a man for the first time when he was thirteen years old, for the last time when he was twenty-nine. At some point he apparently gave up using a real sword but continued to inflict mortal wounds on his adversaries until the end of his fighting career.

The last three decades of Musashi's life were spent refining and teaching his military science. It is said that he never combed his hair, never took a bath, never married, never made a home, and never fathered children. Although he also took up cultural arts, as indeed he recommends to everyone, Musashi himself basically pursued an ascetic warrior's path to the end.

Born into strife, raised in mortal combat, ultimately witness to a transition to peacetime polity on a scale unprecedented in the history of his nation, Miyamoto Musashi abandoned an ordinary life to exemplify and hand on two essential elements of ancient martial and strategic traditions.

The first of these basic principles is keeping inwardly calm and clear even in the midst of violent chaos; the second is not forgetting about the possibility of disorder in times of order. As a warrior of two very different worlds, a world of war and a world of peace, Musashi was obliged to practice both of these fundamental aspects of the warrior's way in a most highly intensified manner, lending to his work a keenness and a ferocity that can hardly be surpassed.

The Book of Family Traditions on the Art of War

The life of Yagyū Munenori (1571–1646) contrasts sharply with that of Miyamoto Musashi, even though both men were professional warriors of the same age. Yagyū received training in martial arts from his father and became the teacher of Tokugawa Hidetada in 1601, when he was barely thirty years old. The Tokugawa Tent Government was established two years later, and Hidetada became the second Shōgun in 1605. Yagyū Munenori was now the official *shōgunke heihō shihan,* or Martial Arts Teacher to the Family of the Shōguns.

Yagyū subsequently distinguished himself in battle in the still unsettled early years of the new Tent Government. In one famous incident when the Shōgun was unexpectedly ambushed, Yagyū personally cut down seven of the attackers with his "killing sword." More and more of the barons and their brothers and sons were now seeking entry into the "New Shadow" school of Yagyū, now a famous warrior and master swordsman.

In spite of his distinguished military career, Yagyū writes of himself that he did not realize the deeper meanings of martial arts until he was already past fifty years old. Miyamoto Musashi, it will be noted, made a similar remark, even though he had been undefeated in his youthful fighting career. Like Musashi, Yagyū also wrote his book on martial arts late in life, after much reflection on his experiences.

The Book of Family Traditions on the Art of War was completed in 1632, the same year that Yagyū Munenori was appointed head of the Secret Service. Under the Tokugawa Tent Government, the role of the Secret Service was to oversee the direct vassals of the Tokugawa Family, police the castle at Edo, oversee the performance of lower-level government officers, watch over official ceremonies, attend the Shōgun, and participate in the high court. Yagyū's writing thus reflects a far more developed social and political consciousness than Musashi's.

The Book of Family Traditions on the Art of War consists of three main scrolls, entitled "The Killing Sword," "The Life-Giving Sword," and "No Sword." These are Zen Buddhist terms adapted to both wartime and peacetime principles of the samurai. The killing sword represents the use of force to quell disorder and eliminate violence. The life-giving sword represents the preparedness to perceive impending problems and forestall them. "No sword" represents the capacity to make full use of the resources of the environment.

Zen and Martial Art

Yagyū's work contains a comparatively large amount of material drawn from Zen Buddhist sources, invoking the similarity between Zen and martial arts on certain points. Yagyū himself makes it clear, however, that the correspondence between Zen and martial arts is imperfect and incomplete, and that he himself has not actually mastered Zen.

Ever since the samurai took power in Japan, centuries before Musashi and Yagyū were born, Buddhists had been trying to civilize and educate the warriors. This does not mean that the samurai caste in general was successfully imbued with Buddhist enlightenment, or even with a Buddhist spirit. One prominent reason for this was that the Buddhists were kept busy, not only trying to civilize the samurai, but also trying to clean up after them and their follies. Buddhism was burdened with the tasks of burying the dead, taking in and raising the many children orphaned by war or poverty or cast off as bastards, and sheltering abused and abandoned wives.

In the relationship between Zen and the samurai, therefore, the teacher should not be assessed by the level of the student. If martial arts were really considered the highest form of study in Japan, as has been suggested by some apologists, Zen masters would have been the students of the warriors, and not the other way around.

The prolonged domination of Japan by the martial caste was an anomaly in human affairs, as reflected by its discord with both native Japanese and greater East

Asian sociopolitical ideals. Because of the way martial rule was established by power, it was fated to bend social and philosophical ideals to its own purposes, rather than submit itself completely to the judgment and guidance of the traditional religions and philosophies it professed to uphold.

THE BOOK
OF FIVE RINGS

Miyamoto Musashi

PREFACE

The science of martial arts called the Individual School of Two Skies is something that I have spent many years refining. Now, wishing to reveal it in a book for the first time, I have ascended Mount Iwato in Higo province of Kyūshū. Bowing to Heaven, paying respects to Kannon, I face the Buddha. I am Shinmen Musashi no Kami, Fujiwara no Genshin, a warrior born in the province of Harima, now sixty years old.

I have set my mind on the science of martial arts since my youth long ago. I was thirteen years old when I had my first duel. On that occasion I won over my opponent, a martial artist named Arima Kihei of the New School of Accuracy. At sixteen years of age I beat a powerful martial artist called Akiyama of Tajima province. When I was twenty-one, I went to the capital city and met martial artists from all over the country. Although I engaged in numerous duels, never did I fail to attain victory.

After that, I traveled from province to province, meeting martial artists of the various schools. Although I dueled more than sixty times, never once did I lose.

That all took place between the time I was thirteen years old and the time I was twenty-nine.

When I had passed the age of thirty and reflected on my experiences, I realized that I had not been victorious because of consummate attainment of martial arts. Perhaps it was because I had an inherent skill for the science and had not deviated from natural principles. It may also have been due to shortcomings in the martial arts of other schools. In any case, I subsequently practiced day and night in order to attain an even deeper principle, and spontaneously came upon the science of martial arts. I was about fifty years old at that time.

Since then I have passed the time with no science into which to inquire. Trusting in the advantage of military science, as I turn it into the sciences of all arts and skills, I have no teacher in anything.

Now, in composing this book, I have not borrowed the old sayings of Buddhism or Confucianism, nor do I make use of old stories from military records or books on military science. With Heaven and Kannon for mirrors, I take up the brush and begin to write, at 4:00 A.M. on the night of the tenth day of the tenth month, 1643.

THE EARTH SCROLL

Martial arts are the warrior's way of life. Commanders in particular should practice these arts, and soldiers must also know this way of life. In the present day there are no warriors with certain knowledge of the way of martial arts.

First let us illustrate the idea of a way of life. Buddhism is a way of helping people, Confucianism is a way of reforming culture. For the physician, healing is a way of life; a poet teaches the art of poetry. Others pursue fortune-telling, archery, or various other arts and crafts. People practice the ways to which they are inclined, developing individual preferences. Few people are fond of the martial way of life.

First of all, the way of warriors means familiarity with both cultural and martial arts. Even if they are clumsy at this, individual warriors should strengthen their own martial arts as much as is practical in their circumstances.

People usually think that all warriors think about is being ready to die. As far as the way of death is concerned, it is not limited to warriors. Mendicants, women, farmers, and even those below them know

their duty, are ashamed to neglect it, and resign themselves to death; there is no distinction in this respect.
The martial way of life practiced by warriors is based on
excelling others in anything and everything. Whether
by victory in an individual duel or by winning a battle
with several people, one thinks of serving the interests
of one's employer, of serving one's own interests, of
becoming well known and socially established. This is
all possible by the power of martial arts.

Yet there will be people in the world who think that
even if you learn martial arts, this will not prove useful
when a real need arises. Regarding that concern, the true
science of martial arts means practicing them in such a
way that they will be useful at any time, and to teach
them in such a way that they will be useful in all things.

ON THE SCIENCE OF MARTIAL ARTS

In China and Japan, practitioners of this science have
been referred to as masters of martial arts. Warriors
should not fail to learn this science.

People who make a living as martial artists these
days only deal with swordsmanship. The priests of the
Kashima and Kantori shrines in Hitachi province have
established such schools, claiming their teachings to
have been transmitted from the gods, and travel around
from province to province passing them on to people;
but this is actually a recent phenomenon.

Among the arts and crafts spoken of since ancient

times, the so-called "art of the advantage" has been included as a craft; so once we are talking about the art of the advantage, it cannot be limited to swordsmanship alone. Even swordsmanship itself can hardly be known by considering only how to win by the art of the sword alone; without question it is impossible to master military science thereby.

As I see society, people make the arts into commercial products; they think of themselves as commodities, and also make implements as items of commerce. Distinguishing the superficial and the substantial, I find this attitude has less reality than decoration.

The field of martial arts is particularly rife with flamboyant showmanship, with commercial popularization and profiteering on the part of both those who teach the science and those who study it. The result of this must be, as someone said, that "amateuristic martial arts are a source of serious wounds."

Generally speaking, there are four walks of life: the ways of the knight, the farmer, the artisan, and the merchant.

First is the way of the farmer. Farmers prepare all sorts of agricultural tools and spend the years constantly attending to the changes in the four seasons. This is the way of the farmer.

Second is the way of the merchant. Those who manufacture wine obtain the various implements required and make a living from the profit they gain according to quality. Whatever the business, merchants make a living from the profits they earn according to their particular status. This is the way of the merchant.

Third, in regard to the warrior knight, that path involves constructing all sorts of weapons and understanding the various properties of weapons. This is imperative for warriors; failure to master weaponry and comprehend the specific advantages of each weapon would seem to indicate a lack of cultivation in a member of a warrior house.

Fourth is the way of the artisan. In terms of the way of the carpenter, this involves skillful construction of all sorts of tools, knowing how to use each tool skillfully, drawing up plans correctly by means of the square and the ruler, making a living by diligent practice of the craft.

These are the four walks of life, of knights, farmers, artisans, and merchants. I will illustrate the science of martial arts by likening it to the way of the carpenter.

The carpenter is used as a metaphor in reference to the notion of a house. We speak of aristocratic houses, military houses, houses of the arts; we speak of a house collapsing or a house continuing; and we speak of such and such a tradition, style, or "house." Since we use the expression "house," therefore, I have employed the way of the master carpenter as a metaphor.

The word for carpenter is written with characters meaning "great skill" or "master plan." Since the science of martial arts involves great skill and master planning, I am writing about it in terms of comparison with carpentry.

If you want to learn the science of martial arts, meditate on this book; let the teacher be the needle, let the student be the thread, and practice unremittingly.

LIKENING THE SCIENCE OF MARTIAL ARTS TO CARPENTRY

As the master carpenter is the overall organizer and director of the carpenters, it is the duty of the master carpenter to understand the regulations of the country, find out the regulations of the locality, and attend to the regulations of the master carpenter's own establishment.

The master carpenter, knowing the measurements and designs of all sorts of structures, employs people to build houses. In this respect, the master carpenter is the same as the master warrior.

When sorting out timber for building a house, that which is straight, free from knots, and of good appearance can be used for front pillars. That which has some knots but is straight and strong can be used for rear pillars. That which is somewhat weak yet has no knots and looks good is variously used for door sills, lintels, doors, and screens. That which is knotted and crooked but nevertheless strong is used thoughtfully in consideration of the strength of the various members of the house. Then the house will last a long time.

Even knotted, crooked, and weak timber can be made into scaffolding, and later used for firewood.

As the master carpenter directs the journeyman, he knows their various levels of skill and gives them appropriate tasks. Some are assigned to the flooring, some to the doors and screens, some to the sills, lintels, and ceilings, and so on. He has the unskilled set out floor joists, and gets those even less skilled to carve wedges. When the master carpenter exercises discernment in the assignment of jobs, the work progresses smoothly.

Efficiency and smooth progress, prudence in all matters, recognizing true courage, recognizing different levels of morale, instilling confidence, and realizing what can and cannot be reasonably expected—such are the matters on the mind of the master carpenter. The principle of martial arts is like this.

The Science of Martial Arts

Speaking in terms of carpentry, soldiers sharpen their own tools, make various useful implements, and keep them in their utility boxes. Receiving instructions from a master carpenter, they hew pillars and beams with adzes, shave floors and shelving with planes, even carve openwork and bas relief. Making sure the measurements are correct, they see to all the necessary tasks in an efficient manner; this is the rule for carpentry. When one has developed practical knowledge of all the skills of the craft, eventually one can become a master carpenter oneself.

An essential habit for carpenters is to have sharp tools and keep them whetted. It is up to the carpenter to use these tools masterfully, even making such things as miniature shrines, bookshelves, tables, lamp stands, cutting boards, and pot covers. Being a soldier is like this. This should be given careful reflection.

Necessary accomplishments of a carpenter are avoiding crookedness, getting joints to fit together, skillful planing, avoiding abrasion, and seeing that there is no subsequent warping.

If you want to learn this science, then take everything I write to heart and think it over carefully.

ON THE COMPOSITION OF THIS BOOK IN FIVE SCROLLS

Distinguishing five courses, in order to explain their principles in individual sections, I have written this book in five scrolls, entitled Earth, Water, Fire, Wind, and Emptiness.

In the Earth Scroll is an outline of the science of martial arts, the analysis of my individual school. The true science cannot be attained just by mastery of swordsmanship alone. Knowing the small by way of the great, one goes from the shallow to the deep. Because a straight path levels the contour of the earth, I call the first one the Earth Scroll.

Second is the Water Scroll. Taking water as the basic point of reference, one makes the mind fluid. Water conforms to the shape of the vessel, square or round; it can be a drop, and it can be an ocean. Water has the color of a deep pool of aquamarine. Because of the purity of water, I write about my individual school in this scroll.

When you attain certain discernment of the principles of mastering swordsmanship, then, when you can defeat one opponent at will, this is tantamount to being able to defeat everyone in the world. The spirit of overcoming others is the same even if there are thousands or tens of thousands of opponents.

The military science of commanders is to construe the large scale from the small scale, like making a monumental icon from a miniature model. Such matters are impossible to write about in detail; to know myriad things by means of one thing is a principle of military science. I write about my individual school in this Water Scroll.

Third is the Fire Scroll. In this scroll I write about battle. Fire may be large or small, and has a sense of violence, so here I write about matters of battle. The way to do battle is the same whether it is a battle between one individual and another or a battle between one army and another. You should observe reflectively, with overall awareness of the large picture as well as precise attention to small details.

The large scale is easy to see; the small scale is hard to see. To be specific, it is impossible to reverse the direction of a large group of people all at once, while the small scale is hard to know because in the case of an individual there is just one will involved and changes can be made quickly. This should be given careful consideration.

Because the matters in this Fire Scroll are things that happen in a flash, in martial arts it is essential to practice daily to attain familiarity, treating them as ordinary affairs, so the mind remains unchanged. Therefore I write about contest in battle in this Fire Scroll.

Fourth is the Wind Scroll. The reason I call this scroll the Wind Scroll is that it is not about my individual school; this is where I write about the various schools of martial arts in the world. As far as using the word wind is concerned, we use this word to mean "style" or "manner" in speaking of such things as ancient style, contemporary style, and the manners of the various houses; so here I write definitively about the techniques of the various schools of martial arts in the world. This is "wind." Unless you really understand others, you can hardly attain your own self-understanding.

In the practice of every way of life and every kind of work, there is a state of mind called that of the deviant. Even if you strive diligently on your chosen path day after day, if your heart is not in accord with it, then even if you think you are on a good path, from the point of view of the straight and true, this is not a genuine path. If you do not pursue a genuine path to its consummation, then a little bit of crookedness in the mind will later turn into a major warp. Reflect on this.

It is no wonder that the world should consider the martial arts to consist solely of swordsmanship. As far as the principles and practices of my martial arts are concerned, this is a distinctly different matter. I write about other schools in this Wind Scroll in order to make the martial arts of the world known.

Fifth is the Emptiness Scroll. The reason this scroll is entitled Emptiness is that once we speak of "emptiness," we can no longer define the inner depths in terms of the surface entryway. Having attained a principle, one detaches from the principle; thus one has spontaneous independence in the science of martial arts and naturally attains marvels: discerning the rhythm when the time comes, one strikes spontaneously and naturally scores. This is all the way of emptiness. In the Emptiness Scroll I have written about spontaneous entry into the true Way.

ON NAMING THIS INDIVIDUAL SCHOOL "TWO SWORDS"

The point of talking about two swords is that it is the duty of all warriors, commanders and soldiers alike, to wear two swords. In olden times these were called *tachi* and *katana*, or the great sword and the sword; nowadays they are called *katana* and *wakizashi*, or the sword and the side arm. There is no need for a detailed discussion of the business of warriors wearing these two swords. In Japan, the way of warriors is to wear them at their sides whether they know anything about them or not. It is in order to convey the advantages of these two that I call my school Two Swords in One.

As for the spear, the halberd, and so on, they are considered extra accoutrements; they are among the tools of the warrior.

For beginners in my school, the real thing is to practice the science wielding both swords, the long sword in one hand and the short sword in the other. When your life is on the line, you want to make use of all your tools. No warrior should be willing to die with his swords at his side, without having made use of his tools. However, when you hold something with both hands, you cannot wield it freely both right and left; my purpose is to get you used to wielding the long sword with one hand.

With large weapons such as the spear and the halberd, there is no choice; but the long and short swords are both weapons that can be held in one hand.

The trouble with wielding the long sword with both hands is that it is no good on horseback, no good when running hurriedly, no good on marshy ground, muddy fields, stony plains, steep roads, or crowded places.

When you have a bow or a spear in your left hand, or whatever other weapon you are wielding, in any case you use the long sword with one hand; therefore, to wield the long sword with both hands is not the true way.

When it is impossible to strike a killing blow using just one hand, then use two hands to do it. It should not require effort. Two Swords is a way to learn to wield the long sword in one hand, whose purpose is first to accustom people to wielding the long sword in one hand.

The long sword seems heavy and unwieldy to everyone at first, but everything is like that when you first take it up: a bow is hard to draw, a halberd is hard to swing. In any case, when you become accustomed to each weapon, you become stronger at the bow, and you acquire the ability to wield the long sword. So when you attain the power of the way, it becomes easy to handle.

To swing the long sword with great velocity is not the right way, as will be made clear in the second section, the Water Scroll. The long sword is to be wielded in spacious places, the short sword in confined spaces; this is the basic idea of the way to begin with.

In my individual school, one can win with the long sword, and one can win with the short sword as well. For this reason, the precise size of the long sword is not fixed. The way of my school is the spirit of gaining victory by any means.

It is better to wield two swords than one long sword when you are battling a mob all by yourself; it is also advantageous when taking prisoners.

Matters such as this need not be written out in exhaustive detail; myriad things are to be inferred from each point. When you have mastered the practice of the science of martial arts, there will be nothing you do not see. This should be given careful and thorough reflection.

On Knowing the Principles of the Words *Martial Arts*

In this path, someone who has learned to wield the long sword is customarily called a martial artist in our society. In the profession of martial arts, one who can shoot a bow well is called an archer, while one who has learned to use a gun is called a gunner. One who has learned to use a spear is called a lancer, while one who has learned to use a halberd is called halberdier.

If we followed this pattern, one who has learned the way of the sword would be called a longswordsman and a sidearmsman. Since the bow, the gun, the spear, and the halberd are all tools of warriors, all of them are avenues of martial arts. Nevertheless, it is logical to speak of martial arts in specific reference to the long sword. Because society and individuals are both ordered by way of the powers of the long sword, therefore the long sword is the origin of martial arts.

When you have attained the power of the long sword, you can singlehandedly prevail over ten men. When it is possible to overcome ten men singlehandedly, then it is possible to overcome a thousand men with a hundred, and to overcome ten thousand men with a thousand. Therefore, in the martial arts of my individual school, it is the same for one man as it is for ten thousand; all of the sciences of warriors, without exception, are called martial arts.

As far as paths are concerned, there are Confucians, Buddhists, tea connoisseurs, teachers of etiquette, dancers, and so on. These things do not exist in the way of warriors. But even if they are not your path, if you have wide knowledge of the ways, you encounter them in everything. In any case, as human beings, it is essential for each of us to cultivate and polish our individual path.

On Knowing the Advantages of Weapons in Martial Arts

In distinguishing the advantages of the tools of warriors, we find that whatever the weapon, there is a time and situation in which it is appropriate.

The side arm, or short sword, is mostly advantageous in confined places, or at close quarters, when you get right up close to an opponent. The long sword generally has appropriate uses in any situation. The halberd seems to be inferior to the spear on a battlefield. The spear is the vanguard, the halberd the rear guard. Given the same degree of training, one with a spear is a bit stronger.

Both the spear and the halberd depend on circumstances; neither is very useful in crowded situations. They are not even appropriate for taking prisoners; they should be reserved for use on the battlefield. They are essential weapons in pitched battle. If you nevertheless learn to use them indoors, focusing attention on petty details and thus losing the real way, they will hardly prove suitable.

The bow is also suitable on the battlefield, for making strategic charges and retreats; because it can be fired rapidly at a moment's notice from the ranks of the lancers and others, it is particularly good for battle in the open fields. It is inadequate, however, for sieging a castle, and for situations where the opponent is more than forty yards away.

In the present age, not only the bow but also the other arts have more flowers than fruit. Such skills are useless when there is a real need.

Inside castle walls, nothing compares to a gun. Even in an engagement in the open fields, there are many advantages to a gun before the battle has begun. Once the ranks have closed in battle, however, it is no longer adequate.

One virtue of the bow is that you can see the trail of the arrows you shoot, which is good. An inadequacy of the gun is that the path of the bullets cannot be seen. This should be given careful consideration.

As for horses, it is essential for them to have powerful stamina and not be temperamental.

Speaking in general terms of the tools of the warrior, one's horse should stride grandly, one's long and short swords should cut grandly, one's spear and halberd should penetrate grandly, and one's bow and gun should be strong and accurate.

You should not have any special fondness for a particular weapon, or anything else, for that matter. Too much is the same as not enough. Without imitating anyone else, you should have as much weaponry as suits you. To entertain likes and dislikes is bad for both commanders and soldiers. Pragmatic thinking is essential.

On Rhythm in Martial Arts

Rhythm is something that exists in everything, but the rhythms of martial arts in particular are difficult to master without practice.

Rhythm is manifested in the world in such things as dance and music, pipes and strings. These are all harmonious rhythms.

In the field of martial arts, there are rhythms and harmonies in archery, gunnery, and even horsemanship. In all arts and sciences, rhythm is not to be ignored.

There is even rhythm in being empty.

In the professional life of a warrior, there are rhythms of rising to office and rhythms of stepping down, rhythms of fulfillment and rhythms of disappointment.

In the field of commerce, there are rhythms of becoming rich and rhythms of losing one's fortune.

Harmony and disharmony in rhythm occur in every walk of life. It is imperative to distinguish carefully between the rhythms of flourishing and the rhythms of decline in every single thing.

The rhythms of the martial arts are varied. First know the right rhythms and understand the wrong rhythms, and discern the appropriate rhythms from among great and small and slow and fast rhythms. Know the rhythms of spatial relations, and know the rhythms of reversal. These matters are specialties of martial science. Unless you understand these rhythms of reversal, your martial artistry will not be reliable.

The way to win in a battle according to military science is to know the rhythms of the specific opponents, and use rhythms that your opponents do not expect, producing formless rhythms from rhythms of wisdom.

With the science of martial arts of my individual school outlined above, by diligent practice day and night the mind is naturally broadened; transmitting it to the world as both collective and individual military science, and I write it down for the first time in these five scrolls entitled Earth, Water, Fire, Wind, and Emptiness.

For people who want to learn my military science, there are rules for learning the art:

1. Think of what is right and true.
2. Practice and cultivate the science.
3. Become acquainted with the arts.
4. Know the principles of the crafts.
5. Understand the harm and benefit in everything.
6. Learn to see everything accurately.
7. Become aware of what is not obvious.
8. Be careful even in small matters.
9. Do not do anything useless.

Generally speaking, the science of martial arts should be practiced with such principles in mind. In this particular science, you can hardly become a master of martial arts unless you can see the immediate in a broad context. Once you have learned the principle, you should not be defeated even in individual combat against twenty or thirty opponents.

First of all, keep martial arts on your mind, and work diligently in a straightforward manner; then you can win with your hands, and you can also defeat people by seeing with your eyes. Furthermore, when you refine your practice to the point where you attain freedom of the whole body, then you can overcome people by means of your body. And since your mind is trained in this science, you can also overcome people by means of mind. When you reach this point, how could you be defeated by others?

Also, large-scale military science is a matter of winning at keeping good people, winning at employing large numbers of people, winning at correctness of personal conduct, winning at governing nations, winning at taking care of the populace, winning at carrying out customary social observances. In whatever field of endeavor, knowledge of how to avoid losing out to others, how to help oneself, and how to enhance one's honor, is part of military science.

THE WATER SCROLL

The heart of the individual Two Skies school of martial arts is based on water; putting the methods of the art of the advantage into practice, I therefore call this the Water Scroll, in which I write about the long sword system of this individual school.

It is by no means possible for me to write down this science precisely as I understand it in my heart. Yet, even if the words are not forthcoming, the principles should be self-evident. As for what is written down here, every single word should be given thought. If you think about it in broad outlines, you will get many things wrong.

As for the principles of martial arts, although there are places in which I have written of them in terms of a duel between two individuals, it is essential to understand in terms of a battle between two armies, seeing it on a large scale.

In this way of life in particular, if you misperceive the path even slightly, if you stray from the right way, you fall into evil states.

The science of martial arts is not just a matter of reading these writings. Taking what is written here personally, do not think you are reading or learning, and do not make up an imitation; taking the principles as if they were discovered from your own mind, identify with them constantly and work on them carefully.

State of Mind in Martial Arts

In the science of martial arts, the state of mind should remain the same as normal. In ordinary circumstances as well as when practicing martial arts, let there be no change at all—with the mind open and direct, neither tense nor lax, centering the mind so that there is no imbalance, calmly relax your mind, and savor this moment of ease thoroughly so that the relaxation does not stop its relaxation for even an instant.

Even when still, your mind is not still; even when hurried, your mind is not hurried. The mind is not dragged by the body, the body is not dragged by the mind. Pay attention to the mind, not the body. Let there be neither insufficiency nor excess in your mind. Even if superficially weakhearted, be inwardly stronghearted, and do not let others see into your mind. It is essential for those who are physically small to know what it is like to be large, and for those who are physically large to know what it is like to be small; whether you are physically large or small, it is essential to keep your mind free from subjective biases.

Let your inner mind be unclouded and open, placing your intellect on a broad plane. It is essential to polish the intellect and mind diligently. Once you have sharpened your intellect to the point where you can see whatever in the world is true or not, where you can tell whatever is good or bad, and when you are experienced in various fields and are incapable of being fooled at all by people of the world, then your mind will become imbued with the knowledge and wisdom of the art of war.

There is something special about knowledge of the art of war. It is imperative to master the principles of the art of war and learn to be unmoved in mind even in the heat of battle.

PHYSICAL BEARING IN MARTIAL ARTS

As for physical appearance, your face should not be tilted downward, upward, or to the side. Your gaze should be steady. Do not wrinkle your forehead, but make a furrow between your eyebrows. Keep your eyes unmoving, and try not to blink. Narrow your eyes slightly. The idea is to keep a serene expression on your face, nose straight, chin slightly forward.

The back of the neck should be straight, with strength focused in the nape. Feeling the whole body from the shoulders down as one, lower the shoulders, keep the spine straight, and do not let the buttocks stick out. Concentrate power in the lower legs, from the knees down through the tips of the feet. Tense the abdomen so that the waist does not bend.

There is a teaching called "tightening the wedge," which means that the abdomen is braced by the scabbard of the short sword in such a manner that the belt does not loosen.

Generally speaking, it is essential to make your ordinary bearing the bearing you use in martial arts, and make the bearing you use in martial arts your ordinary bearing. This should be given careful consideration.

Focus of the Eyes in Martial Arts

The eyes are to be focused in such a way as to maximize the range and breadth of vision. Observation and perception are two separate things; the observing eye is stronger, the perceiving eye is weaker. A specialty of martial arts is to see that which is far away closely and to see that which is nearby from a distance.

In martial arts it is important to be aware of opponents' swords and yet not look at the opponents' swords at all. This takes work.

This matter of focusing the eyes is the same in both small- and large-scale military science.

It is essential to see to both sides without moving the eyeballs.

Things like this are hard to master all at once when you're in a hurry. Remember what is written here, constantly accustom yourself to this eye focus, and find out the state where your eye focus does not change no matter what happens.

Gripping the Long Sword

In wielding the long sword, the thumb and forefinger grip lightly, the middle finger grips neither tightly nor loosely, while the fourth and little fingers grip tightly. There should be no slackness in the hand.

The long sword should be taken up with the thought that it is something for killing opponents. Let there be no change in your grip even when slashing opponents; make your grip such that your hand does not flinch. When you strike an opponent's sword, block it, or pin it down, your thumb and forefinger alone should change somewhat; but in any case you should grip your sword with the thought of killing.

Your grip when cutting something to test your blade and your grip when slashing in combat should be no different, gripping the sword as you would to kill a man.

Generally speaking, fixation and binding are to be avoided, in both the sword and the hand. Fixation is the way to death, fluidity is the way to life. This is something that should be well understood.

On Footwork

In your footwork, you should tread strongly on your heels while allowing some leeway in your toes. Although your stride may be long or short, slow or fast, according to the situation, it is to be as normal. Flighty steps, unsteady steps, and stomping steps are to be avoided.

Among the important elements of this science is what is called complementary stepping; this is essential. Complementary stepping means that you do not move one foot alone. When you slash, when you pull back, and even when you parry, you step right-left-right-left, with complementary steps. Be very sure not to step with one foot alone. This is something that demands careful examination.

Five Kinds of Guard

The five kinds of guard are the upper position, middle position, lower position, right-hand guard, and left-hand guard. Although the guard may be divided into five kinds, all of them are for the purpose of killing people. There are no other kinds of guard besides these five.

Whatever guard you adopt, do not think of it as being on guard; think of it as part of the act of killing.

Whether you adopt a large or small guard depends on the situation; follow whatever is most advantageous.

The upper, middle, and lower positions are solid guards, while the two sides are fluid guards. The right and left guards are for places where there is no room overhead or to one side. Whether to adopt the right or left guard is decided according to the situation.

What is important in this path is to realize that the consummate guard is the middle position. The middle position is what the guard is all about. Consider it in terms of large-scale military science: the center is the seat of the general, while following the general are the other four guards. This should be examined carefully.

The Way of the Long Sword

To know the Way of the long sword means that even when you are wielding your sword with two fingers, you know just how to do it and can swing it easily.

When you try to swing the long sword fast, you deviate from the Way of the long sword, and so it is hard to swing. The idea is to swing the sword calmly, so that it is easy to do.

When you try to swing a long sword fast, the way you might when using a fan or a short sword, you deviate from the Way of the long sword, so it is hard to swing. That is called "short sword mincing" and is ineffective for killing a man with a long sword.

When you strike downward with the long sword, bring it back up in a convenient way. When you swing it sideways, bring it back sideways, returning it in a convenient way. Extending the elbow as far as possible and swinging powerfully is the Way of the long sword.

Procedures of Five Formal Techniques

First Technique

In the first technique, the guard is in the middle position, with the tip of the sword pointed at the opponent's face. When you close ranks with the opponent, and the opponent strikes with the long sword, counter by deflecting it to the right. When the opponent strikes again, you hit the point of his sword back up; your sword now having bounced downward, leave it as it is until the opponent strikes again, whereupon you strike the opponent's hands from below.

These five formal techniques can hardly be understood just by writing about them. The five formal techniques are to be practiced with sword in hand. By means of these five outlines of swordplay, you will know my science of swordplay, and the techniques employed by opponents will also be evident. This is the point of telling you that there are no more than five guards in the Two Sword method of swordsmanship. Training and practice are imperative.

Second Technique

In the second technique of swordplay, the guard is in the upper position, and you strike the opponent at the very same time as the opponent tries to strike you. If your sword misses the opponent, leave it there for the moment, until the opponent strikes again, whereupon you strike from below, sweeping upward. The same principle applies when you strike once more.

Within this technique are various states of mind and various rhythms. If you practice the training of my individual school by means of what lies within this technique, you will gain thorough knowledge of the five ways of swordplay and will be able to win under any circumstances. It requires practice.

Third Technique

In the guard of the third technique, the sword is held in the lower position; with a feeling of taking matters in hand, as the opponent strikes, you strike at his hands from below. As you strike at his hands, the opponent strikes again; as he tries to knock your sword down, bring it up in rhythm, then chop off his arms sideways after he has struck. The point is to strike an opponent down all at once from the lower position just as he strikes. The guard with the sword in the lower position is something that is met with both early on and later on in the course of carrying out this science; it should be practiced with sword in hand.

Fourth Technique

In the guard of the fourth technique, the sword is held horizontally to the left side, to hit the opponent's hands from below when he tries to strike. When the opponent tries to knock down your sword as it strikes upward from below, block the path of his sword just like that, with the idea of hitting his hands, and cut diagonally upward toward your shoulder. This is the way to handle a long sword. This is also the way to win by blocking the path of the opponent's sword if he tries to strike again. This should be considered carefully.

Fifth Technique

In the fifth procedure, the sword is held horizontally to your right side. When you note the location of the opponent's attack, you swing your sword from the lower side diagonally upward into the upper guard position, then slash directly from above. This is also essential for expertise in the use of the long sword. When you can wield a sword according to this technique, then you can wield a heavy long sword freely.

These five formal techniques are not to be written down in detail. To understand the use of the long sword in my school, and also generally comprehend rhythms and discern opponents' swordplay techniques, first use these five techniques to develop your skills constantly. Even when fighting with opponents, you perfect the use of the long sword, sensing the minds of opponents, using various rhythms, gaining victory in any way. This requires careful discernment.

On the Teaching of Having a Position without a Position

Having a position without a position, or a guard without a guard, means that the long sword is not supposed to be kept in a fixed position. Nevertheless, since there are five ways of placing the sword, the guard positions must follow along. Where you hold your sword depends on your relationship to the opponent, depends on the place, and must conform to the situation; wherever you hold it, the idea is to hold it so that it will be easy to kill the opponent.

Sometimes the upper guard position is lowered a bit, so that it becomes the middle position, while the middle guard position may be elevated a bit, depending on the advantage thereof, so that it becomes the upper position. At times the lower guard position is also raised a bit, to become the middle position. The two side-guard positions may also be moved somewhat toward the center, depending on where you are standing vis-à-vis your opponent, resulting in either the middle or lower guard position.

In this way, the principle is to have a guard position without a position. First of all, when you take up the sword, in any case the idea is to kill an opponent. Even though you may catch, hit, or block an opponent's slashing sword, or tie it up or obstruct it, all of these moves are opportunities for cutting the opponent down. This must be understood. If you think of catching, think of hitting, think of blocking, think of tying up, or think of obstructing, you will thereby become unable to make the kill. It is crucial to think of everything as an opportunity to kill. This should be given careful consideration.

In large-scale military science, the arraying of troops is also a matter of positioning. Every instance thereof is an opportunity to win in war. Fixation is bad. This should be worked out thoroughly.

Striking Down an Opponent in a Single Beat

Among the rhythms used to strike an opponent, there is what is called a single beat. Finding a position where you can reach the opponent, realizing when the opponent has not yet determined what to do, you strike directly, as fast as possible, without moving your body or fixing your attention.

The stroke with which you strike an opponent before he has thought of whether to pull back, parry, or strike is called the single beat. Once you have learned this rhythm well, you should practice striking the intervening stroke quickly.

The Rhythm of the Second Spring

The rhythm of the second spring is when you are about to strike and the opponent quickly pulls back or parries; you feint a blow, and then strike the opponent as he relaxes after tensing. This is the stroke of the second spring.

It will be very difficult to accomplish this stroke just by reading this book. It is something that you understand all of a sudden when you have received instruction.

Striking without Thought and without Form

When your opponent is going to strike, and you are also going to strike, your body is on the offensive, and your mind is also on the offensive; your hands come spontaneously from space, striking with added speed and force. This is called striking without thought or form, and is the most important stroke. This stroke is encountered time and time again. It is something that needs to be learned well and refined in practice.

THE FLOWING WATER STROKE

The flowing water stroke is used when you are going toe to toe with an opponent, when the opponent tries to pull away quickly, dodge quickly, or parry your sword quickly: becoming expansive in body and mind, you swing your sword from behind you in an utterly relaxed manner, as if there were some hesitation, and strike with a large and powerful stroke.

Once you have learned this stroke, it is certainly easy to strike. It is essential to discern the opponent's position.

THE CHANCE HIT

When you launch an offensive and the opponent tries to stop it or parry it, you strike at his head, hands, and feet with one stroke. Striking wherever you can with one swoop of the long sword is called the chance hit. When you learn this stroke, it is one that is always useful. It is something that requires precise discernment in the course of dueling.

The Spark Hit

The spark hit is when your opponent's sword and your sword are locked together and you strike as strongly as possible without raising your sword at all. One must strike quickly, exerting strength with the legs, torso, and hands.

This blow is hard to strike without repeated practice. If you cultivate it to perfection, it has a powerful impact.

The Crimson Foliage Hit

The idea of the crimson foliage hit is to knock the opponent's sword down and take the sword over. When an opponent is brandishing a sword before you, intending to strike, hit, or catch, you strike the opponent's sword strongly, your striking mood that of "striking without thought and without form," or even "spark hitting." When you then follow up closely on that, striking with the sword tip downward (*kissakisagari*), your opponent's sword will inevitably fall.

If you cultivate this blow to perfection, it is easy to knock a sword down. It must be well practiced.

The Body Instead of the Sword

The body in this sense can also be called the body that takes the place of the sword. In general, when you take the offensive, your sword and your body are not launched simultaneously. Depending on your chances of striking the opponent, you first adopt an offensive posture with your body, and your sword strikes independently of your body.

Sometimes you may strike with your sword without your body stirring, but generally the body goes on the offensive first, followed up by the stroke of the sword. This requires careful observation and practice.

Striking and Hitting

By striking and hitting, I mean two different things. The sense of striking is that whatever stroke you employ, you make a deliberate and certain strike. Hitting means something like running into someone. Even if you hit an opponent so hard that he dies on the spot, this is a hit. A strike is when you consciously and deliberately strike the blow you intend to strike. This requires examination and reflection.

To hit an opponent on the hands or legs means to hit first, in order to make a powerful strike after hitting. To hit means something like "feel out." If you really learn to master this, it is something extraordinary. It takes work.

The Body of the Short-Armed Monkey

The posture of the short-armed monkey means not reaching out with your hand. The idea is that when you close in on an opponent, you get in there quickly, before the opponent strikes, without putting forth a hand at all.

When you intend to reach forth, your body invariably pulls back; so the idea is to move the whole body quickly to get inside the opponent's defense. It is easy to get in from arm's length. This should be investigated carefully.

The Sticky Body

The sticky body means getting inside and sticking fast to an opponent. When you get inside the opponent's defenses, you stick tight with your head, body, and legs. The average person gets his head and legs in quickly, but the body shrinks back. Sticking to an opponent means that you stick so close that there is no gap between your bodies. This should be investigated carefully.

Comparing Height

Comparing height means that when you close in on an opponent, under whatever circumstances, you extend your legs, waist, and neck, so that your body does not contract; closing in powerfully, you align your face with the opponent's, as if you were comparing height and proving to be the taller of the two. The essential point is to maximize your height and close in strongly. This requires careful work.

Gluing

When your opponent and you both strike forth, and your opponent catches your blow, the idea is to close in with your sword glued to the opponent's sword. Gluing means that the sword is hard to get away from; you should close in without too much force. Sticking to the opponent's sword as if glued, when you move in close it does not matter how quietly you move in.

There is gluing and there is leaning. Gluing is stronger than leaning. These things must be distinguished.

The Body Blow

The body blow is when you close in on an opponent's side and hit him with your body. Turning your face slightly to the side and thrusting your left shoulder forward, you hit him in the chest.

In making the hit, exert as much strength as possible with your body; in making the hit, the idea is to close in with a bound at the moment of peak tension.

Once you have learned to close in like this, you can knock an opponent several yards back. It is even possible to hit an opponent so hard that he dies.

This requires thorough training and practice.

Three Parries

When you attack an opponent, in order to parry the blow of the opponent's sword, making as if to stab him in the eyes, you dash his sword to your right with your sword, thus parrying it.

There is also what is called the stabbing parry. Making as if to stab the opponent in the right eye, with the idea of clipping off his neck, you parry the opponent's striking sword with a stabbing thrust.

Also, when an opponent strikes and you close in with a shorter sword, without paying so much attention to the parrying sword, you close in as if to hit your opponent in the face with your left hand.

These are the three parries. Making your left hand into a fist, you should think of it as if you were punching your opponent in the face. This is something that requires thorough training and practice.

Stabbing the Face

When you are even with an opponent, it is essential to keep thinking of stabbing him in the face with the tip of your sword in the intervals between the opponent's sword blows and your own sword blows. When you have the intention of stabbing your opponent in the face, he will try to get both his face and his body out of the way. When you can get your opponent to shrink away, there are various advantages of which you can avail yourself to win. You should work this out thoroughly.

In the midst of battle, as soon as an opponent tries to get out of the way, you have already won. Therefore it is imperative not to forget about the tactic of "stabbing the face." This should be cultivated in the course of practicing martial arts.

Stabbing the Heart

Stabbing the heart is used when fighting in a place where there is no room for slashing, either overhead or to the sides, so you stab the opponent. To make the opponent's sword miss you, the idea is to turn the ridge of your sword directly toward your opponent, drawing it back so that the tip of the sword does not go off kilter, and thrusting it into the opponent's chest.

This move is especially for use when you are tired out, or when your sword will not cut. It is imperative to be able to discern expertly.

The Cry

A cry and a shout are used whenever you launch an attack to overcome an opponent and the opponent also strikes back; coming up from below as if to stab the opponent, you strike a counterblow.

In any case, you strike with a cry and a shout in rapid succession. The idea is to thrust upward with a cry, then strike with a shout.

This move is one that can be used anytime in a duel. The way to cry and shout is to raise the tip of the sword with the sense of stabbing, then slashing all at once, immediately upon bringing it up. The rhythm must be practiced well and examined carefully.

The Slapping Parry

When you are exchanging blows with an opponent in a duel, you hit the opponent's sword with your own sword as he strikes; this is called the slapping parry. The idea of the slapping parry is not to hit particularly hard, nor to catch and block; responding to the opponent's striking sword, you hit the striking sword, then immediately strike the opponent.

It is essential to be the first to hit and the first to strike. If the rhythm of your parrying blow is right, no matter how powerfully an opponent strikes, as long as you have any intention at all of hitting, your sword tip will not fall. This must be learned by practice and carefully examined.

A Stand against Many Opponents

A stand against many opponents is when an individual fights against a group. Drawing both long and short swords, you hold them out to the left and right, extending them horizontally. The idea is that even if opponents come at you from all four sides, you chase them into one place.

Discerning the order in which opponents attack, deal with those who press forward first; keeping an eye on the whole picture, determining the stands from which opponents launch their attacks, swinging both swords at the same time without mutual interference, it is wrong to wait. The idea is to immediately adopt the ready position with both swords out to the sides and, when an opponent comes forth, to cut in with a powerful attack, overpower him, then turn right away to the next one to come forth and slash him down.

Intent on herding opponents into a line, when they seem to be doubling up, sweep right in powerfully, not allowing a moment's gap.

It will be hard to make headway if you only chase opponents around en masse. Then again, if you think about getting them one after another as they come forth, you will have a sense of waiting and so will also have a hard time making headway. The thing is to win by sensing the opponents' rhythms and knowing where they break down.

If you get a group of practitioners together from time to time and learn how to corner them, it is possible to take on one opponent, or ten, or even twenty opponents, with peace of mind. It requires thorough practice and examination.

Advantage in Dueling

Advantage in dueling means understanding how to win using the long sword according to the laws of martial arts. This cannot be written down in detail; one must realize how to win by practice. This is the use of the long sword that reveals the true science of martial arts; it is transmitted by word of mouth.

The Single Stroke

This means to gain victory with certainty by the accuracy of a single stroke. This cannot be comprehended without learning martial arts well. If you practice this well, you will master martial arts, and this will be a way to attain victory at will. Study carefully.

The State of Direct Penetration

The mind of direct penetration is something that is transmitted when one receives the true path of the school of Two Swords. It is essential to practice well, so as to train the body to this military science. This is transmitted orally.

Epilogue

The above is an overall account of the arts of swordsmanship in my individual school, which I have recorded in this scroll.

In military science, the way to learn how to take up the long sword and gain victory over others starts with using the five formal techniques to learn the five kinds of guard position, then learning how to wield a long sword and gain total freedom of movement, sharpening the mind to discern the rhythms of the path, and taking up the sword oneself. When you are able to maneuver your body and feet however you wish, you beat one person, you beat two people, and you come to know what is good and what is bad in martial arts.

Studying and practicing each item in this book, fighting with opponents, you gradually attain the principles of the science; keeping it in mind at all times, without any sense of hurry, learning its virtues whenever the opportunity arises, taking on any and all opponents in duels, learning the heart of the science, even though it is a path of a thousand miles, you walk one step at a time.

Thinking unhurriedly, understanding that it is the duty of warriors to practice this science, determine that today you will overcome your self of the day before, tomorrow you will win over those of lesser skill, and later you will win over those of greater skill. Practicing in accord with this book, you should determine not to let your mind get sidetracked.

No matter how many opponents you beat, as long as you do anything in contravention of training, it cannot be the true path. When this principle comes to mind, you should understand how to overcome even dozens of opponents all by yourself. Once you can do that, you should also be able to grasp the principles of large-scale and individual military science by means of the power of knowledge of the art of the sword.

This is something that requires thorough examination, with a thousand days of practice for training and ten thousand days of practice for refinement.

THE FIRE SCROLL

In the military science of the individual Two Sword school, combat is thought of as fire. Matters pertaining to victory and defeat in combat are thought of as a scroll of fire and so are written down herein.

To begin with, people of the world all think of the principles of advantage in martial arts in small terms. Some know how to take advantage of a flick of the wrist, using the tips of the fingers. Some know how to win using a fan, by a timely movement of the forearm. Then again, using a bamboo sword or something like that, they may just learn the minor advantage of speed, training their hands and feet in this way, concentrating on trying to take advantage of a little more speed.

As far as my military science is concerned, I have discerned the principles of living and dying through numerous duels in which I set my life on the line, learning the science of the sword, getting to know the strength and weakness of opponents' sword blows, comprehending the uses of the blade and ridge of the sword, and practicing how to kill opponents. In the course of doing this, little sissy things never even occurred to me.

Especially when one is in full combat gear, one does not think of small things.

Furthermore, to fight even five or ten people singlehandedly in duels with your life on the line and find a sure way to beat them is what my military science is all about. So what is the difference between the logic of one person beating ten people and a thousand people beating ten thousand people? This is to be given careful consideration.

Nevertheless, it is impossible to collect a thousand or ten thousand people for everyday practice to learn this science. Even if you are exercising alone with a sword, assess the knowledge and tactics of all adversaries, know the strong and weak moves of adversaries, find out how to beat everyone by means of the knowledge and character of military science, and you will become a master of this path.

Who in the world can attain the direct penetration of my military science? Training and refining day and night with the determination to eventually consummate it, after having perfected it, one gains a unique freedom, spontaneously attains wonders, and is endowed with inconceivable powers of penetration. This is how cosmic law is carried out through martial arts.

The Physical Situation

In discerning the lay of the physical situation, there is what is known as positioning yourself with the sun at your back. This means that you take up your stance with the sun behind you. If the situation does not allow you to keep the sun at your back, then you should strive to keep the sun to your right.

This also applies indoors, where you should keep the light to your back, or to your right. It is desirable to be sure that there is nothing in the way behind you, and that there is plenty of room to your left, taking a stance in such a way as to cut off the space to your right and close in.

At night also, where you can see your opponents, take your stand with fires to your back and lights to your right, as indicated above.

In order to "look down on the enemy," understand that you should take your stand on the highest ground, even if it is only slightly elevated. Indoors, the seat of honor should be regarded as the high ground.

Anyway, when it comes to battle, the idea is to chase opponents to your left; it is essential to make sure that obstacles are to the rear of your opponents, then chase them into an obstacle any way you can.

When you get opponents to an obstacle, in order to prevent them from observing the situation, press your attack without letup so that they cannot look around. The same thing about not letting opponents observe the situation also applies indoors, when you are chasing them into doorsills, head jambs, doors, screens, verandas, pillars, or other obstacles.

In any case, the direction in which you chase opponents should be toward places where the footing is bad or there is obstruction on either side. Use whatever qualities of the setting you can, concentrating on taking advantage of the situation. This is something that calls for careful and thorough reflection and practice.

Three Preemptions

There are three kinds of preemption. One is when you preempt by attacking an opponent on your own initiative; this is called preemption from a state of suspension. Another is when you preempt an opponent making an attack on you; this is called preemption from a state of waiting. Yet another is when you and an opponent attack each other simultaneously; this is called preemption in the state of mutual confrontation.

These are the three ways of preemption. At the beginning of any battle, there are no other choices but these three initiatives. Since it is a matter of gaining victory quickly by preemption, therefore preemption is the foremost concern in martial arts.

There are many details involved in preemption, but they cannot be fully written down because it is a matter of putting priority on the pattern of the particular time, perceiving the intention of opponents, and using your knowledge of martial arts to win.

First there is preemption from a state of suspension. When you want to attack, you remain calm and quiet, then get the jump on your opponent by attacking suddenly and quickly. You can preempt by being outwardly powerful and swift while inwardly leaving reserves. You can also get the jump by steeling your mind to the utmost, accelerating your pace a bit, and making a violent attack the instant you get up close to the opponent. You can also win by letting your mind go free, determining to beat your opponent at the same thing from start to finish, gaining victory by thoroughgoing strength of heart. All of these are examples of preemption from a state of suspension.

Second is preemption from a state of waiting. When an opponent comes at you, you do not react but appear to be weak: then, when the opponent gets near, you spring away with a powerful leap, almost as if you were flying; then, when you see the opponent slack, you forcefully overcome him straightaway. This is one way of preemption. Also, when an opponent attacks and you aggressively meet the attack, the moment you sense a chance in the rhythm of the opponent's attack, you can gain victory right then and there. This is the principle of preemption from a state of waiting.

Third is preemption in a state of mutual confrontation. In case an opponent attacks swiftly, you attack calmly yet powerfully; when the opponent gets close, tighten your bearing with absolute resolve, and when the opponent shows signs of slacking, overcome him with force immediately. Then again, when an opponent attacks calmly and quietly, accelerate your own attack slightly, with your body lightly buoyant; when the opponent gets close, clash once and then, adapting to his condition, overcome him forcefully. This is preemption in a state of mutual confrontation.

These moves are hard to write about in detail; they should be worked out along the general lines of the moves written down here. These three ways of preemption depend on the time and logic of the situation. Even though you are not to be always the one to attack, if it amounts to the same thing, you would rather take the initiative and put opponents on the defensive.

However it may be, the idea of preemption is gaining certain victory through the power of knowledge of martial arts. It must be cultivated and refined very thoroughly.

Holding Down the Pillow

Holding down the pillow means not letting someone raise his head. In martial arts, in the course of dueling, it is bad to be maneuvered around by others. It is desirable to maneuver opponents around freely, by whatever means you may.

Therefore opponents will be thinking along these lines, and you too have this intention, but it is impossible to succeed in this without comprehending what others are doing.

Martial arts include stopping an opponent's striking blows, arresting his thrusts, tearing away his grips. Holding down the pillow means that when you have attained my science in reality and are engaged with an opponent, whenever the opponent evinces any sign of intending to make a move, you perceive it before he acts. Stopping an opponent's attack at the initial outset, not letting him follow through, is the sense of "holding down the pillow."

For example, you inhibit an opponent's attack from the letter *a*, so to speak; you inhibit an opponent's leap from the letter *l*, and inhibit an opponent's cut from the letter *c*. These are all the same idea.

Whenever opponents try to attack you, let them go ahead and do anything that is useless, while preventing them from doing anything useful. This is essential to military science.

Here, if you consciously try to thwart opponents, you are already late. First, doing whatever you do scientifically, thwart the opponent's very first impulse to try something, thus foiling everything. To manipulate opponents in this way is mastery of the art of war, which comes from practice. The act of holding down the pillow requires thorough examination.

Crossing a Ford

When you cross a sea, there are places called straits. Also, places where you cross a sea even twelve or fifteen miles wide are called fords. In going through the human world as well, in the course of a lifetime there will be many points that could be called crossing a ford.

On the sea lanes, knowing where the fords are, knowing the state of the boat, knowing the weather, even without launching companion boats, you adapt to the state of the time, sometimes taking advantage of crosswinds, sometimes even getting favorable winds, knowing that even if the wind changes you can still reach port by oar, you take command of the ship and cross the ford.

With that attitude, in passing through the human world you should also have a sense of crossing a ford in an emergency.

In martial arts, in the midst of battle, it is also essential to "cross the ford." Sensing the state of opponents, aware of your own mastery, you cross the ford by means of the appropriate principles, just as a skilled captain goes over a sea-lane.

Having crossed over the ford, furthermore, there is peace of mind.

To "cross a ford," put the adversary in a weak position and get the jump yourself; then you will generally quickly prevail. Whether in large-scale military science or individual martial arts, the sense of crossing a ford is essential. It should be savored thoroughly.

Knowing the State of Affairs

In large-scale military science, knowing the state of affairs means discerning the flourishing and decline of the opponent, discerning the intentions of adversary troops and perceiving their condition, clearly seeing the state of affairs, determining how to deploy your own troops so as to gain certain victory by the principles of military science, and doing battle with knowledge of what lies ahead.

Also, in individual martial arts, you determine opponents' traditions, observe the personal character of adversaries, find out people's strengths and weaknesses, maneuver in ways contrary to opponents' expectations, determine opponents' highs and lows, ascertain the rhythms in between, and make the first move; this is essential.

If your own power of insight is strong, the state of affairs of everything will be visible to you. Once you have attained complete independent mastery of martial arts, you will be able to figure out the minds of opponents and thus find many ways to win. This demands work.

Stomping a Sword

Stomping a sword is a move used only in martial arts. First of all, in large-scale military science, even with bows and guns, when opponents attack you with whatever they have, after they have shot their first volley and are renewing their barrage, it is hard for you to make your attack if you are cocking a bow or loading a gun. The idea is to attack quickly while the enemy is in the process of shooting.

The sense of this is that if you attack quickly, it is hard to use arrows against you, hard to shoot you with a gun. The idea is that whatever opponents attack with, you immediately sense the pattern and gain victory by stomping down anything the opponent does.

In the context of individual martial arts as well, if you strike in the wake of an opponent's striking sword, it will turn into a clashing, clanging volley of blows, and you will get nowhere. When an opponent lashes out with his sword, you overpower his assault by stomping the sword down with your foot, seeing to it that he cannot strike a second blow.

Stomping is not only done with the feet. You should also learn to "stomp" with your body, "stomp" with your mind, and of course "stomp" with a sword, in such a way as to prevent opponents from making a second move.

This means getting the jump on everything. It does not mean randomly hitting an opponent with the idea of settling the contest all at once. It means instantaneous and unyielding follow-up. This should be investigated thoroughly.

Knowing Disintegration

Disintegration is something that happens to everything. When a house crumbles, a person crumbles, or an adversary crumbles, they fall apart by getting out of rhythm with the times.

In large-scale military science, it is also essential to find the rhythm of opponents as they come apart and pursue them so as not to let openings slip by. If you miss the timing of vulnerable moments, there is the likelihood of counterattack.

In individual martial arts it also happens that an adversary will get out of rhythm in combat and start to fall apart. If you let such a chance get by you, the adversary will recover and thwart you. It is essential to follow up firmly on any loss of poise on the part of an opponent, to prevent him from recovering.

The follow-up calls for directness and power; it is a matter of lashing out violently in such a way that an opponent cannot recover. This lashing out must be carefully analyzed. If you do not let go, there is a sense of slovenliness. This is something that requires work.

Becoming the Opponent

Becoming the opponent means you should put yourself in an opponent's place and think from the opponent's point of view.

As I see the world, if a burglar holes up in a house, he is considered a powerful opponent. From his point of view, however, the whole world is against him; he is holed up in a helpless situation. The one who is holed up is a pheasant; the one who goes in there to fight it out is a hawk. This calls for careful reflection.

In large-scale military science as well, opponents are thought of as powerful and dealt with carefully. When you have good troops, know the principles of martial arts well, and sense the way to overcome an opponent, you need not worry.

You should also put yourself in the opponent's position in individual martial arts. When one meets a master of the science, someone who comprehends martial arts and is good at the science, one thinks one will lose. Consider this well.

Letting Go Four Hands

Letting go four hands is for when you and an opponent are in a deadlock and no progress is being made in the fight. It means that when you think you are going to get into a deadlock, you stop that right away and seize victory by taking advantage of a different approach.

In large-scale military science as well, if there is total deadlock and no progress is being made, there will be a loss of personnel. It is essential to stop right away and seize victory by taking advantage of a tactic unsuspected by the enemy.

In individual martial arts also, if you think you are getting into a deadlock, then it is essential to immediately change your approach, ascertain the opponent's state, and determine how to win by means of a very different tactic.

MOVING SHADOWS

Moving shadows is something you do when you cannot discern what an adversary is thinking.

In large-scale military science, when you cannot discern the enemy's state, you pretend to make a powerful attack to see what they will do. Having seen opponents' methods, it is easy to seize victory by taking advantage of different tactics specially adapted to each case.

In individual martial arts also, when an opponent is brandishing his sword behind him or to his side, when he is suddenly about to strike, he shows his intent in his sword. Once it shows perceptibly, you should immediately sense the advantage and know how to win with certainty. If you are inattentive, you will miss the rhythm. This should be examined thoroughly.

ARRESTING SHADOWS

Arresting shadows is something you do when adversaries' aggressive intentions toward you are perceptible.

In large-scale military science, this means to arrest the enemy's action at the point of the very impulse to act. If you demonstrate strongly to opponents how you control the advantage, they will change their minds, inhibited by this strength. You change your attitude too—to an empty mind, from which you take the initiative and seize victory.

In individual martial arts as well, you use an advantageous rhythm to arrest the powerful determination of the adversary's motivation; then you find the winning advantage in the moment of pause and now take the initiative. This must be worked out thoroughly.

INFECTION

There is infection in everything. Even sleepiness can be infectious, and yawning can be infectious. There is even the infection of a time.

In large-scale military science, when adversaries are excited and evidently are in a hurry to act, you behave as though you are completely unfazed, giving the appearance of being thoroughly relaxed and at ease. Do this, and adversaries themselves are influenced by this mood, becoming less enthusiastic.

When you think opponents have caught that mood, you empty your own mind and act quickly and firmly, thus to gain the winning advantage.

In individual martial arts as well, it is essential to be relaxed in body and mind, notice the moment an opponent slackens, and quickly take the initiative to win.

There is also something called "entrancing" that is similar to infection. One entrancing mood is boredom.

Another is restlessness. Another is faintheartedness. This should be worked out thoroughly.

Upset

Upset happens in all sorts of things. One way it happens is through a feeling of being under acute pressure. Another is through a feeling of unreasonable strain. A third is through a feeling of surprise at the unexpected.

In large-scale military science, it is essential to cause upset. It is critical to attack resolutely where enemies are not expecting it; then, while their minds are unsettled, use this to your advantage to take the initiative and win.

In individual martial arts also, you appear relaxed at first, then suddenly charge powerfully; as the opponent's mind changes pitch, it is essential that you follow what he does, not letting him relax for a moment, perceiving the advantage of the moment and discerning right then and there how to win. This must be investigated diligently.

Threat

There is fright in everything. This means being frightened by the unexpected.

Even in large-scale military science, threatening an adversary is not something right before the eyes. You may threaten by sound, you may threaten by making the small seem large, and you may threaten by making an unexpected move from the side. These are situations in which fright occurs. If you can seize the moment of fright, you can take advantage of it to gain victory.

In individual martial arts also, you can threaten by means of your body, you can threaten by means of your sword, and you can threaten by means of your voice. What is essential is to suddenly make a move totally unexpected by the opponent, pick up on the advantage of fright, and seize victory right then and there. This must be worked out thoroughly.

Sticking Tight

Sticking tight means when you are fighting at close range, you and your adversary each exerting great force against the other, and you see that it is not going well, you then stick tight to your opponent; the essential point is to take advantage of opportunities to win even as you wrestle together.

Whether in large- or small-scale military science, when you and opponents have taken sides and are facing off and it is not clear who will prevail, right then and there you stick right to the opponents, so that you cannot be separated, and in that process find the advantage, determine how to win, and seize victory powerfully; this is quintessential. This must be studied diligently.

Coming Up against Corners

Coming up against corners means that when you push something that is strong, it hardly gives way immediately, just like that.

In large-scale military science, observe the opposing troops; where they have surged ahead, hit the corner of this strong front, and you should get the advantage.

As the corner collapses, everyone gets the feeling of collapse. Even as they are collapsing, it is essential to realize when each corner is ready to go and sense when to overcome it.

In individual martial arts too, when you inflict pain on part of his body each time an opponent makes an aggressive move, his body will weaken by degrees until he is ready to collapse and it is easy to beat him.

It is essential to study this carefully to discern where you can win.

Flustering

Flustering opponents means acting in such a way as to prevent them from having a steady mind.

In large-scale military science, this means that you assess adversaries' minds on the battlefield and use the power of your knowledge of the art of war to manipulate their attention, making them think confusing thoughts about what you are going to do. It means finding a rhythm that will fluster adversaries, accurately discerning where you can win.

In individual martial arts as well, you try various maneuvers according to the opportunity of the moment, making the opponent think you are now going to do this, now that, now something else, until you find the opponent starting to get flustered, and thus you win at will. This is the essence of battle; it should be studied very carefully.

Three Shouts

The three shouts are called the initial, middle, and final shout. The essential point is to call out in accord with the situation. Because a shout is forceful, we shout in emergencies like fires and squalls; the voice shows force and power.

In large-scale military science, at the beginning of battle the shouting should be as loud as possible, in the course of battle the shouting should be low-pitched and booming from the depths, while after victory the shouting should be loud and strong. These are the three shouts.

In individual martial arts, you feint and shout in order to stir the opponent, then lash out after your cry. You also shout after having struck an opponent down, with a cry signaling victory. These are called before and after shouts.

You never shout at the same time as you swing your sword. When you shout in the midst of battle, you use the sound to mount a rhythm, crying out in a low pitch.

Mixing

In the context of large-scale combat, mixing means that when two groups are facing off and your opponents are strong, you attack one of the opponents' flanks, as if to mix in with them; then, when you see the opponents crumble, you leave off and attack again where they are strong. In general, the idea is to attack in a winding zigzag.

This is also essential in the context of individual martial arts, when you face a group of adversaries singlehandedly. Each time you have finished one off or driven one off, again you attack a strong one, finding the opponents' rhythm, zigzagging left and right in a suitable rhythm, observing the condition of the adversary so as to attack effectively.

When you have found an enemy's range and are going to cut through, the principle of the advantage is to seize victory forcefully, without any reservations. This state of mind also applies to a situation when you are closing in on a powerful opponent in individual combat.

The sense of mixing is to plunge right in without any hesitation in your steps. This should be distinguished carefully.

CRUSHING

Crushing requires a crushing mood, as when you view an opponent as weak and become strong yourself, thus overwhelming your adversary.

In large-scale military science, this means you look down upon an enemy whose numbers are small, or even if there are many of them, when opponents are demoralized and weakening, you concentrate your force on crushing them, thus mowing them down.

If your crushing is weak, it can backfire. You have to carefully distinguish the state of mind in which you are fully in control as you crush.

In the context of individual martial arts too, when your opponent is not as skilled as you are, or when his rhythm is fouled up, or when he starts to back off, it is essential not to let him catch his breath. Mow him right down without even giving him time to blink his eyes. The most important thing is not to let him recover.

This should be studied very carefully.

MOUNTAIN AND SEA CHANGING

"Mountain and sea" means that it is bad to do the same thing over and over again. You may have to repeat something once, but it should not be done a third time.

When you try something on an opponent, if it does not work the first time, you will not get any benefit out of rushing to do it again. Change your tactics abruptly, doing something completely different. If that still does not work, then try something else.

Thus the science of martial arts involves the presence of mind to act as the sea when the enemy is like a mountain, and act as a mountain when the enemy is like a sea. This requires careful reflection.

Knocking the Heart Out

When you fight with an adversary and appear to win by your skill in this science, your opponent may still have ideas and, while appearing to be beaten, still inwardly refuse to acknowledge defeat. Knocking the heart out is for such cases.

This means that you suddenly change your attitude to stop the enemy from entertaining any such ideas; so the main thing is to see that adversaries feel defeated from the bottom of their hearts.

You can knock the heart out of people with weapons or with your body or with your mind. It is not to be understood in just one way.

When your enemies have completely lost heart, you do not have to pay attention to them anymore. Otherwise, you remain mindful. As long as adversaries still have ambitions, they will hardly collapse.

In both large- and small-scale martial arts, knocking the heart out should be practiced thoroughly.

Becoming New

When fighting with enemies, if you get to feeling snarled up and are making no progress, you toss your mood away and think in your heart that you are starting everything anew. As you get the rhythm, you discern how to win. This is "becoming new."

Anytime you feel tension and friction building up between yourself and others, if you change your mind that very moment, you can prevail by the advantage of radical difference. This is "becoming new."

In large-scale military science, it is essential to understand becoming new. It is something that suddenly appears through the power in knowledge of martial arts. This must be well considered.

Small and Large

When you are fighting adversaries and get to feeling snarled up in petty maneuvers, remember this rule of military science: while in the midst of minutiae, suddenly you shift to a large perspective.

Changing to great or small is an intentional part of the science of the art of war. It is essential for warriors to seek this even in the ordinary consciousness of human life. This mentality is critical to military science, whether large or small scale.

This concern should be given careful consideration.

A Commander Knowing Soldiers

"A commander knowing soldiers" is a method always practiced in times of conflict after having reached the mastery to which one aspires. Having attained the power in the knowledge of the arts of war, you think of your adversaries as your own soldiers, understanding that you should do with them as you wish, intending to manipulate them freely. You are the commander, the opponents are the troops. This takes work.

Letting Go of the Hilt

"Letting go of the hilt" has various meanings. It has the meaning of winning without a sword, and it also has the meaning of failing to win with a sword. The various different senses cannot be written down but call for thorough training and practice.

Being Like a Rock Wall

"Being like a rock wall" is when a master of martial arts suddenly becomes like a rock wall, inaccessible to anything at all, immovable. This is transmitted by word of mouth.

Epilogue

What is written above consists entirely of things that constantly come to mind in the course of practicing the art of swordsmanship of my individual school. Because

I am now writing these principles down for the first time, they are somewhat mixed up in terms of order, and it is hard to define them in detail. Nevertheless, they can be guidelines for people who are supposed to learn this science.

I have concentrated on martial arts since youth, training my hands and body to the mastery of swordsmanship, getting into all sorts of various states of mind. What I see on inquiry into other schools is that some are pretentious talkers, and some perform fancy maneuvers with their hands; even though they may look good to people, there is surely no true heart there at all.

Of course, it may seem as if people are training body and mind even when they are practicing such things, but they become sicknesses of the path, persistent and hard to get rid of; they are bases of the decay of the straight path of martial arts in the world, and of the abandonment of the Way.

For the art of swordsmanship to be a real science, such as to win victory in battle with adversaries, no change whatsoever is to be made in these principles. When you attain the power of knowledge of my military science and put it into practice in a straightforward manner, there can be no doubt of victory.

THE WIND SCROLL

Military science involves knowledge of the methods of other schools. Here in this Wind Scroll, I have written about the various other schools of martial arts. Unless you know the ways of other schools, you certainly cannot understand the way of my individual school.

What I see on inquiry into others' martial arts is that some schools use large long swords and concentrate on power in their moves. Some practice their science using a short long sword they call a "little long sword." There are also schools that contrive many moves with the long sword, calling the positions of the sword the formal techniques and transmitting the science as the inner teaching.

In this scroll I will clearly expose the fact that none of these are the real Way, thus to let it be known what is good and what bad, what true and what false. The principle of my individual school is something distinctly different. Other schools become theatrical, dressing up and showing off to make a living, commercializing martial arts; therefore it would seem that they are not the true Way.

Furthermore, martial art is conventionally viewed in a limited way, as if it consisted only of swordsmanship. Do you think you have realized how to attain victory just by learning to wield a long sword and training your body and hands? This is not a certain way in any case.

I have exposed each of the deficiencies of other schools in this book. The point is to examine carefully and savor thoroughly, to come to an understanding of the advantages of the individual school of Two Swords.

ON WIELDING EXTRA-LONG SWORDS IN OTHER SCHOOLS

There are some other schools that are fond of extra-long swords. From the point of view of my martial art, I see them as weak schools. The reason for this is that these other schools do not know about prevailing over others by any means necessary; considering the length of the sword its virtue, they must want their swords to be extra long so that they can beat opponents from a distance.

The conventional saying about winning by even an inch in reach is something that refers to people who know nothing about martial arts. Therefore, to try to win from a distance by an advantage in sword length without knowing the principles of martial arts is something that people do because of weakness of heart. That is why I consider this weak martial art.

At times when you are engaged with an opponent at close quarters, the longer your sword is, the harder it is to strike with it; you cannot swing the sword back and forth enough, and it becomes a burden. Then you are in a worse situation than someone wielding a small sidearm sword.

For those who prefer extra-long swords, they have their own reason, but it is logical for themselves alone; from the point of view of the real Way of the world, it is illogical. Will you necessarily lose if you use a shorter long sword and not an extra-long sword?

And suppose the physical situation is such that above, below, and/or the sides are blocked; or suppose the social situation is one where only side arms are worn; to wish for an extra-long sword under these conditions is a bad attitude, because it is to doubt the science of martial arts.

Furthermore, there are people who lack the requisite physical strength.

Since ancient times it has been said that the great includes the small, so it is not a matter of indiscriminately disliking length; it is a matter of disliking the attitude of bias in favor of length.

In the context of large-scale military science, an extra-long sword is a large contingent, a shorter one is a small contingent. Is a battle between a small contingent and a large contingent impossible? There are many examples of a small contingent winning over a large contingent. Thus in my individual school there is an aversion to a narrow, biased attitude. This calls for careful examination.

POWERFUL SWORD BLOWS IN OTHER SCHOOLS

There should be no such thing as strong sword blows or weak sword blows. A swing of a sword made with the intention to swing powerfully is rough, and you can hardly win by roughness alone.

Furthermore, if you slash with unreasonable force when you are going to kill someone, intending to deal a powerful blow of the sword, you will not be successful.

Even when you are making a test cut on a dummy or something, it is wrong to try deliberately to slash powerfully.

When facing an enemy in mortal combat, nobody thinks of striking weakly or powerfully. When one only thinks of killing the other, there is no sense of strength, and of course no sense of weakness; one only thinks of the death of the enemy.

If you hit someone else's sword strongly using an extra-powerful swing, it will turn out badly because of excessive force. If you hit someone else's sword forcefully, your own sword will be delayed.

So there is no such thing as a particularly powerful sword blow. Even in large-scale military science, if you have a powerful contingent wishing to gain a forceful victory in battle, the fact is that your opponent also has powerful people and wants to fight forcefully. In that respect, both are the same. When it comes to winning victory in everything, it is impossible to prevail without reason.

In my school, no consideration is given to anything unreasonable; the heart of the matter is to use the power of the knowledge of martial arts to gain victory any way you can. This must be worked out thoroughly.

The Use of Shorter Long Swords in Other Schools

To think of winning by means of a shorter long sword alone is not the true Way. Since ancient times long and short swords have been distinguished in terminology.

Physically powerful people can wield even a large sword with ease, so there is no point in unreasonable fondness for a shorter sword. The reason for this is that spears and halberds are also carried to make use of their length. The idea that you are going to use a shorter long sword to cut through, plunge in, and seize an opponent in the interval between swings of his sword is biased and therefore wrong.

Furthermore, when you watch out for gaps, everything else is neglected, and there comes to be a sense of entanglement, which is to be avoided. And if you try to use a short weapon to penetrate the enemy's defense and take over, that will not be of any use when in the midst of numerous opponents.

Even if you think that what you gain from a shorter weapon is the ability to cut through a crowd, leap freely, and whirl around, in each case you are in a defensive mode of swordplay and are thus in a distracted state of mind. This is not a reliable way to go.

You might just as well chase people around in a powerful and straightforward manner, making people jump out of the way, contriving to throw them into confusion, taking the route that aims solely at certain victory.

This logic also applies to large-scale military science. All else being equal, you might as well take a large contingent, attack the enemy all of a sudden, and destroy them at once. This attitude is the focus of military science.

What people of the world ordinarily study when they practice martial arts is to parry, deflect, get away, and get through safely; therefore their minds are drawn by this method and wind up being maneuvered and manipulated by others. Since the Way of martial arts is direct and straightforward, the intent to stalk and overcome people rightly is essential. This should be considered carefully.

Numerous Sword Strokes in Other Schools

When an excessive number of sword moves are taught, it must be to commercialize the art and impress beginners with knowledge of many moves with a sword. This attitude is to be avoided in military science.

The reason for this is that it is delusion to think that there are all sorts of ways of cutting people down. In the matter of cutting people down, there are no different ways in the world. Whether or not one is knowledgeable, and even if one is a woman or a child, there are not so many ways to strike and cut; if there are variants, they are no more than stabbing and slashing.

To begin with, since the point is killing, there is no reason for there to be a large number of ways to do it. Even so, depending on the situation, according to events, in cases where there is obstruction in the surroundings, such as above or to the sides, there have to be five positions so that there is a way to wield a sword without getting stuck.

To add anything else, things like cutting an opponent down with a twist of the hands, a twirl of the body, or a leap to a distance, are not the true way. To cut someone down, you cannot cut them down by twisting or twirling; these are useless things.

In my military science, it is essential that the physical aspect and the mental state both be simple and direct, gaining victory by causing opponents to strain distortedly and go off kilter, causing the hearts of adversaries to do the twisting and twirling. This should be examined carefully.

POSITIONS OF THE SWORD IN OTHER SCHOOLS

It is wrong to concentrate solely on the guard position of the sword. Whenever there are guard positions in the world, it must be when there are no opponents.

The reasoning behind this is that to set up standard rules as customary standards or current rules is not feasible in the course of actually contesting for victory. The thing is to contrive to put the adversary at a disadvantage.

Whatever the point of reference, the adoption of a guard position has the sense of making use of immovability. To guard a castle, or to array a battle line in a defensive position, has the sense of being strong and unaffected even under attack; this is the normal meaning.

In the course of struggle for victory by military science, the thing is to concentrate on seizing the initiative and getting the jump on others in everything. The sense of a guard or defensive posture is that of awaiting the initiative. This should be worked out thoroughly.

In the course of struggle for victory by military science, you win by disrupting others' defenses, by making moves opponents do not expect, by confusing opponents, or irritating them, or scaring them, sensing the pattern of the rhythm when opponents get mixed up to seize victory. Thus there is an aversion to the defensive attitude involved in concern with guard positions. Therefore in my science there is what is called having a guard without a guard, meaning that one has a defense without being defensive.

In large-scale military science also, the main concern for a pitched battle is to learn how many troops the adversary has, note the lay of the battleground, know the state of your own troops, marshal their best qualities, rally them, and only then start to fight.

There is a totally different feeling in being attacked by others first than in attacking others yourself. The sense of being able to wield a sword well enough to catch and parry an opponent's blows is tantamount to taking your spear and halberd and sticking them in the ground as fence posts. When you are going to strike an adversary, in contrast, you can even pull up a fence post and use it as you would a spear or halberd. This is something that should be examined carefully.

The Focus of the Eyes in Other Schools

The focus of the eyes depends on the school: there are those who fix their eyes on the opponent's sword, and there are also those who fix their eyes on the opponent's hands; there are those who fix their eyes on the opponent's face, and there are also those who fix their eyes on the opponent's feet, and so on. When you try to fix your eyes on some particular point, there is a sense of distraction, and this becomes what is known as an affliction in martial arts.

People playing football may not keep their eyes on the ball, yet they can still steal it away with a kick and dribble it around, because when one is thoroughly practiced in something, it is not necessary to look deliberately. In the arts of jugglers too, when they are practiced in the techniques, they can balance a door on the nose and juggle several swords at once, all without deliberately watching; since they are involved in practice all the time, they see what is going on spontaneously.

In the context of the science of martial arts as well, when you become familiar with each adversary, perceive the degree of seriousness of people's minds, and are able to practice the science effectively, you can see even the distance and speed of a sword. Generally speaking, the focus of the eyes in martial arts is on the hearts and minds of the people involved.

When it comes to large-scale military science, the eyes are also focused on the state of the opposing troops.

Of two ways of perception, observing and seeing, the observing eye is stronger, perceiving the heart and mind of the adversary, seeing the state of the situation, focusing the eyes broadly, perceiving the conditions for battle, perceiving the strength and weakness of the occasion, concentrating on seizing victory with precision.

Whether in large- or small-scale military science, there is no narrow focus of the vision. As I have already written, by finicky narrowness of focus, you forget about bigger things and get confused, thus letting certain victory escape you. This principle demands careful reflection and thorough practice.

Footwork in Other Schools

There are various ways of quick-stepping, such as those known as the floating step, the leaping step, the springing step, the stomping step, the crow step, and so on. From the point of view of my martial art, all of these seem deficient.

The reason why I dislike the floating step is that one's steps are in any case likely to become unsteady in battle, so the proper course is to stride as surely as possible.

The reason I do not like the leaping step is that there is a sense of excitement in the leaping and a sense of fixation on leaping. Since there is no reason to leap over and over again, a leaping step is bad.

Also, the springing step is ineffective because there is a sense of bounding. The stomping step is a passive stance and is especially objectionable.

Other than these, there are also various quick-steps such as the crow step.

Since you may engage opponents in marshes or swamps, or in mountains and rivers, or on rocky plains, or on narrow roads, depending on the place, there are situations in which it is impossible to leap and spring or to quick-step.

In my martial art, there is no change in footwork; it is just like walking along a road as usual. Following the rhythm of the opponent, finding the right physical position in conditions of both hurry and calm, the stride should be orderly, without slack or excess.

In large-scale military science as well, footwork is critical. The reason for this is that if you attack indiscriminately without knowing the intentions of your adversary, you will miss the rhythm and find it hard to win. Also, if you are striding calmly and do not notice when opponents are demoralized and crumbling, you will let victory elude you and will be unable to effect a quick settlement of the contest.

It is essential to perceive discouragement and crumbling, then overwhelm adversaries by not letting them relax for even a moment. This requires thorough training and practice.

The Use of Speed in Other Schools

In martial arts, speed is not the true Way. As far as speed is concerned, the question of fast or slow in anything derives from failure to harmonize with the rhythm.

When you master an art or science, your performance does not appear to be fast. For example, there are professional courier runners who travel a route of about fifteen miles; but even so, they do not run fast from morning to night. As for those who lack the training, even if they seem to run all day, they do not reach the goal.

In the art of the dance, if a poor singer accompanies the song of a skilled singer, there is a sense of lag, which results in haste. Also, when "Old Pine" is played on the drums, it is a quiet piece, but in this case too, someone who is unskilled will tend to fall behind or get ahead. And while "High Dunes" has a rapid tempo, it is wrong to perform it too fast.

As the saying goes, the fast one stumbles and fails to get there on time. Of course, being too slow and too late is also bad.

The performance of an expert seems relaxed but does not leave any gaps. The actions of trained people do not seem rushed. The principle of the Way can be known from these illustrations.

Speed is particularly bad in the context of the science of martial arts. The reasons for this are as follows. Here too, depending on the place, say for example in a bog, it is impossible to move and run fast. With a long sword, there is no such thing as killing with greater speed; unlike with a fan or short sword, if you try to cut quickly, you will not be able to cut at all. This calls for careful discernment.

In large-scale military science as well, the feeling of speed and hurry is bad. With the attitude of "holding down the pillow," there is no being slow.

Furthermore, when people speed rashly, it is essential for you to be the reverse, becoming calm and quiet, not being drawn in by them. The way to work on this state of mind requires training and practice.

The Esoteric and Exoteric in Other Schools

In the context of matters of martial arts, what is to be called exoteric, what is to be called esoteric? Depending on the art, there are esoteric transmissions of the ultimate realization that are passed on as inner oral traditions, but when it comes to the principle of dueling with opponents, it is not a matter of fighting exoterically and killing esoterically.

My way of teaching martial arts is to have beginners learn and practice those of the techniques that are easily mastered, first teaching them the principles that they will readily understand. As for those things that their minds have a hard time reaching, I observe the understanding of each individual, subsequently teaching them deeper principles gradually, step by step. Even so, since I generally make them learn such things as have actual relevance to addressing these matters, there is no such thing as a distinction between the esoteric and the exoteric.

So it is in the world, when you go into the depths of the mountains, if you want to go farther, you will again come out of the mountains. In any art or science, there is that for which secrecy or reserve is appropriate, and that which may well be spoken of openly. But when it comes to the principles of war, what is to be hidden, what is to be revealed?

Accordingly, in transmitting my science, I do not care for written pledges or articles of penalties. Observing the intellectual power of students, teaching them a straight path, having them abandon the bad aspects of the "five ways" or "six ways" of martial arts, so that they naturally enter into the real science of warriors, causing their minds to be free from doubt—this is the way I teach martial arts. Thorough training and practice are necessary.

Epilogue

In the preceding nine articles on the martial arts of other schools, where I have written their outlines in this Wind

Scroll, although it is imperative to write clearly about each school, from the initiation to the inner lore, I do not make a point of writing the names of which particular secret of which particular school I am referring to.

The reason for this is that the views of each school, and the logic of each path, are realized differently according to the individual person, depending on the mentality; so even in the same school there are some slight differences of understanding. Thus for the sake of posterity I have not recorded the particular schools to which I refer.

Having divided the general run of other schools into nine categories, when we look from the point of view of the right way for the world, from the point of view of straightforward human reason, things such as preferences for extra-long or extra-short swords, preferences for force or yielding, concern with crudeness and fineness, are all biased paths; so even if I do not reveal them as the initiatory or inner lore of other schools, everybody should know about them.

In my individual school, there is no such thing as a distinction between initiatory and inner lore about the long sword. There is no such thing as the ultimate guard. It is only a matter of understanding its effective qualities in your heart and mind; this is what is essential to martial art.

THE SCROLL OF EMPTINESS

In writing about the science of martial arts of the individual school of Two Swords in the Scroll of Emptiness, the meaning of emptiness is that the realm where nothing exists, or cannot be known, is seen as empty.

Of course, emptiness does not exist. Knowing of nonexistence while knowing of existence is emptiness.

Wrongly viewed among people of the world, not understanding anything is itself considered emptiness. This is not real emptiness; it is all delusion.

In the context of this science of martial arts as well, in carrying out the way as a warrior, not knowing the laws of warriors is not emptiness; being confused, one may call a state of helplessness emptiness, but this is not real emptiness.

Warriors learn military science accurately and go on to practice the techniques of martial arts diligently. The way that is practiced by warriors is not obscure in the least. Without any confusion in mind, without slacking off at any time, polishing the mind and attention, sharpening the eye that observes and the eye that sees, one should know real emptiness as the state where there is no obscurity and the clouds of confusion have cleared away.

As long as they do not know the real Way, whether in Buddhism or in worldly matters, everybody may think their path is sure and is a good thing, but from the point of view of the straight way of mind, seen in juxtaposition with overall social standards, they turn away from the true Way by the personal biases in their minds and the individual warps in their vision.

Knowing that mentality, taking straightforwardness as basic, taking the real mind as the Way, practicing martial arts in the broadest sense, thinking correctly, clearly, and comprehensively, taking emptiness as the Way, you see the Way as emptiness.

In emptiness there is good but no evil. Wisdom exists, logic exists, the Way exists, mind is empty.

12 May 1645

NOTES

p. 3 *Two Skies* is one name for Musashi's school of
martial arts, which he referred to as the individual school of Two Skies or Two Swords.

p. 3 *Kannon* is one of the most popular of Buddhist
icons, representing the activity of universal
compassion. Kannon happens to be the icon of
the temple where Musashi went into retreat;
there is no indication that he had any particular
devotion to Kannon.

p. 6 The *Kashima* and *Kantori* shrines in eastern
Japan were dedicated to war. The Kashima
Shrine propitiates the god Takemikazuchi-no-
mikoto, worshiped as a god of war since ancient
times. The cult of this shrine was important
in the early Japanese conquest of the largest
of the islands in antiquity. The Kashima New
School of Accuracy, a school of martial arts as-
sociated with this shrine, was said to have been
founded in the time of the prehistorical sixteenth emperor, Nintoku Tennō, who built
Mozunomimihara-no-naka-no-misasagi, the

largest mound tomb in the world. The Kashima New School of Accuracy is attributed to an ancient descendent of the god Kuninatsu-o-ookashima-no-mikoto. The Ka(n)tori Shrine propitiates the god Futsunushi-no-kami. This shrine is reputed to have been established in the time of Jimmu Tennō, the first emperor of Japan, whose name Jimmu means Divine Warrior. A school of martial arts called the Katori Shinto School, or the Katori School of the Divine Sword (the two names are homonyms), was founded as recently as 1940.

p. 30 *Five kinds of guard.* The word for "guard," *kamae*, comes from the verb *kamaeru*, which means to build, set up, adopt a (usually defensive) stance, posture, or attitude. In social parlance, when someone *kamaeru*, that means the person becomes defensive in attitude. The related verb *kamau* means to take trouble over someone or something, to make a fuss.

p. 62 *Infection.* The celebrated pianist Josef Hofmann taught that a performer should convey excitement to an audience by means of the performer's memory of excitement, not by actually becoming excited oneself. This is a sublime example of the principle of infection.

p. 62 *The infection of a time.* The mentality or mood of a time or an era dominates more effectively by infection than it could by overt persuasion or coercion, because the source and nature of the infection are not obvious.

p. 87 *Five ways or six ways of martial arts.* Here Musashi refers to stylistic embellishment for its own sake, in contrast to the fundamental practicalities of the art of war.

THE BOOK OF
FAMILY TRADITIONS ON
THE ART OF WAR

Yagyū Munenori

THE KILLING SWORD

There is an old saying, "Weapons are instruments of ill omen, despised by the Way of Heaven. To use them only when unavoidable is the Way of Heaven." The reason weapons are instruments of ill omen is that the Way of Heaven is the Way that gives life to beings, so something used for killing is truly an instrument of ill omen. Thus the saying has it that what contradicts the Way of Heaven is despised.

Nevertheless, it also says that to use arms when unavoidable is also the Way of Heaven. What does this mean? Although flowers blossom and greenery increases in the spring breeze, when the autumn frost comes, leaves always drop and trees wither. This is the judgment of nature.

This is because there is logic in striking down something when it is completed. People may take advantage of events to do evil, but when that evil is complete, it is attacked. That is why it is said that using weapons is also the Way of Heaven.

It may happen that myriad people suffer because of the evil of one man. In such a case, myriad people are saved by killing one man. Would this not be a true example of "the sword that kills is the sword that gives life"?

There is a science to the use of arms. If you try to kill someone without knowing the science, you will probably get killed yourself.

On careful reflection, in matters of martial arts, the martial art involved in one-on-one sword dueling has but one winner and one loser. This is extremely small martial art, and what is gained or lost by winning or losing is trifling.

When the whole land wins with one individual's victory, and the whole land loses with one individual's loss, this is martial art on a large scale. The one individual is the commander, the whole land is the military forces. The forces are the hands and feet of the commander. To work the forces well is to get the hands and feet of the commander to work well. If the forces do not work, that means the hands and feet of the commander do not work.

Just as one faces off with two swords, operating the great function of the great potential, using one's hands and feet skillfully so as to gain victory, in the same way the martial art of the commander, properly speaking, is to successfully employ all forces and skillfully create strategies so as to win in war.

Furthermore, while it is a matter of course to go out on the field of combat to determine victory and defeat when two battle formations are pitched against each other, one who is a commander pitches two battle formations in his chest, mentally leaning a great army into battle; this is the art of war in the mind.

Not forgetting about disturbance when times are peaceful is an art of war. Seeing the situation of states, knowing when there will be disruption, and healing disturbance before it happens, is also the art of war.

When a country is pacified, the consideration given to the selection of officials and the security of the nation is also a martial art. When officials pursue personal interest and thus oppress the common people, this above all is the beginning of the end for a nation. To observe the situation carefully, planning in such a way as to avoid letting the state perish through the self-seeking of officials, is like watching an opponent in a duel to see his move before he makes it. Should one not observe with utmost attention? This is what makes martial art a matter of such great potential.

Also, surrounding rulers, there are treacherous people who pretend to be righteous when in the presence of superiors yet have a glare in their eyes when they look at subordinates. Unless these people are bribed, they present the good as bad, so the innocent suffer and the guilty gloat. To see the potential for this happening is even more urgent than to notice a concealed scheme.

The country is the ruler's country, the people are the ruler's people. Those who serve the ruler personally are subjects of the ruler just as are those who serve at a remove. How far apart is their distance? They are like hands and feet in the service of the ruler. Are the feet any different from the hands just because they are farther away? Since they both feel pain and itch the same, which can be called nearer, which farther away?

Therefore people will resent even an honest ruler if those close to the ruler bleed those far away and cause the innocent to suffer.

There are only a few people close to a ruler, perhaps five or ten. The majority of people are remote from rulers. When many people resent their ruler, they will express their feelings. Now, when those close to the ruler have all along been after their own interests, and not acting in consideration of the ruler, and therefore serve in such a way that the people resent the ruler, when the time comes, those close to the ruler will be the first to set upon him.

This is the doing of those close to the ruler, not the personal fault of the ruler. It is desirable that the potential for such situations be clearly perceived and that those distant from the rulership not be excluded from its benefits.

Also, in social and professional relationships, since you are acting as you see situations develop, the attitude is the same as that of the warrior, even when there is no discord. The mindfulness to observe the dynamic of situations even in a group is an art of war.

If you do not see the dynamic of a situation, you may remain too long in company where you should not be and get into trouble for no reason. When people say things without seeing others' states of mind, thus getting into arguments, even forfeiting their lives as a result, this is all a matter of the difference between seeing or not seeing the dynamic of a situation and the states of the people involved.

Even to furnish a room so that everything is in the right place is to see the dynamic of a situation. Thus it involves something of the mindfulness of the warrior's art.

Indeed, although the phenomena may differ, the principle is the same. Therefore it can even be applied accurately to the affairs of state.

It is bias to think that the art of war is just for killing people. It is not to kill people, it is to kill evil. It is a strategy to give life to many people by killing the evil of one person.

What is written in these three scrolls is a book that does not go outside of the house. Nevertheless, that does not mean the Way is secret. Secrecy is for the sake of conveying knowledge. If knowledge is not conveyed, that is tantamount to there being no book. Let my descendents think on this well.

The Great Learning

It is said that The Great Learning is the gate of elementary learning. Whenever you go to a house, first you go in through the gate. Therefore the gate is a sign that you have reached the house. Going through this gate, you enter the house and meet the host.

Learning is the gate to attainment of the Way. Therefore learning is the gate, not the house. When you see the gate, do not think it is the house. You have to go through the gate to get to the house, which is inside, behind it.

Since learning is a gate, when you read books do not think this is the Way. This misconception has made many people remain ignorant of the Way no matter how much they study or how many words they know. Even if you can read as fluently as a commentary of an ancient, if you are unaware of the principles, you cannot make the Way your own.

Nevertheless, even though this is so, it is also hard to reach the Way without learning. It is also hard to say that someone understands the Way simply by virtue of being learned and articulate. There are some people who naturally conform to the Way without learning how.

The Great Learning speaks of consummating knowledge and perfecting things. Consummating knowledge means knowing the principles of everything that people in the world know. Perfecting things means that when you know the principle of everything thoroughly, then you know everything and can do everything. When there is nothing more you know, there is nothing you can do either. When you do not know the principle, nothing at all comes to fruition.

In all things, uncertainty exists because of not knowing. Things stick in your mind because of being in doubt. When the principle is clarified, nothing sticks in your mind. This is called consummating knowledge and perfecting things. Since there is no longer anything sticking in your mind, all your tasks become easy to do.

For this reason, the practice of all the arts is for the purpose of clearing away what is on your mind. In the beginning, you do not know anything, so paradoxically you do not have any questions on your mind and you are obstructed by that. This makes everything difficult to do.

When what you have studied leaves your mind entirely, and practice also disappears, then, when you perform whatever art you are engaged in, you accomplish the techniques easily without being inhibited by concern over what you have learned, and yet without deviating from what you have learned. This is spontaneously conforming to learning without being consciously aware of doing so. The science of the art of war can be understood through this.

To learn all the sword strokes, the physical postures, and the focus of the eyes, to thoroughly learn all there is to learn and practice it, is the spirit of consummating knowledge. Then, when you have succeeded in learning, when everything you have learned disappears from your conscious mind and you become innocent, this is the spirit of perfecting things.

When you have built up achievement in cultivation of learning and practice, even as your hands, feet, and body act, this does not hang on your mind. You are detached from your learning yet do not deviate from your learning. Whatever you do, your action is free.

At this time, you do not even know where your own mind is; neither the celestial devil nor outsiders can spy into your heart. The learning is for the purpose of reaching this state. Once you have learned this successfully, learning disappears.

This is the ultimate sense and the progressive transcendentalism of all the Zen arts. Forgetting learning, relinquishing mind, harmonizing without any self-conscious knowledge thereof, is the ultimate consummation of the Way.

This stage is a matter of entering from learning into no learning.

Mood and Will

The mind with a specific inward attitude and an intensive concentration of thought is called will. Will being within, what emanates outwardly is called mood.

To give an illustration, the will is like the master of

a house, while the mood is like a servant. The will is within, employing the mood.

If the mood rushes out too much, you will stumble. You should have your will restrain your mood, so that it does not hurry.

In the context of martial arts, lowering the center of gravity can be called will. Facing off to kill or be killed can be called the mood. Lower your center of gravity securely, and do not let your mood become hurried and aggressive. It is essential to control your mood by means of your will, calming down so that your will is not drawn by your mood.

Appearance and Intention

Appearance and intention are fundamental to the art of war. Appearance and intention mean the strategic use of ploys, the use of falsehood to gain what is real.

Appearance and intention inevitably ensnare people when artfully used, even if people sense that there is an ulterior intention behind the overt appearance. When you set up your ploys and opponents fall for them, then you win by letting them act on your ruse.

As for those who do not fall for a ploy, when you see they will not fall into one trap, you have another one set. Then, even if opponents have not fallen for your original ploy, in effect they actually have.

In Buddhism this is called expedient means. Even though the real truth is hidden inside while strategy is employed outwardly, when you are finally led into the real truth, the pretenses now all become real truth.

In the spirit religion, there is what is called the mystery of the spirits. The mystery is kept secret in order to foster religious faith. When people have faith, they and others benefit from it.

In the warrior's way, this is called strategy. Although strategy is falsehood, when the falsehood is used in order to win without hurting people, the falsehood finally becomes true. This is an example of what is called achieving harmonious order by means of its contrary.

BEATING THE GRASS TO SCARE THE SNAKES

There is something in Zen called "beating the grass to scare the snakes." To startle or surprise people a little is a device, like hitting at snakes in the grass to scare them.

To do something unexpected as a ploy to startle an opponent is also an appearance concealing an ulterior intention, an art of war.

When an opponent is startled and the feeling of opposition is distracted, the opponent will experience a gap in reaction time.

Even simple, ordinary gestures like raising your hand are used to distract an opponent's attention.

Throwing down your sword is also an art of war. If you have attained mastery of swordlessness, you will never be without a sword. The opponent's sword is your sword. This is acting at the vanguard of the moment.

The Vanguard of the Moment

The vanguard of the moment is before the opponent has begun to make a move. This first impulse of movement is the energy, feeling, or mood, held back in the chest. The dynamic of the movement is energy, feeling, or mood. To accurately see an opponent's energy, feeling, and mood, and to act accordingly in their presence, is called the vanguard of the moment.

This effective action is a specialty of Zen, where it is referred to as the Zen dynamic.

The energy, feeling, or mood hidden within and not revealed is called the potential of the moment. It is like a hinge, which is inside the door. To see the invisible workings hidden inside, and to act upon that, is called the art of war at the vanguard of the moment.

Aggressive and Passive Modes

The aggressive mode is when you attack intently, slashing with extreme ferocity the instant you face off, aggressively seeking to get in the first blow.

The feeling of aggression is the same whether it is in the mind of the opponent or in your own mind.

The passive mode is when you do not attack precipitously but wait for the opponent to make the first move. Being extremely careful should be understood as a passive mode.

The aggressive and passive modes refer to the distinction between attacking and waiting.

Logical Principles of Aggressive and Passive Attitudes of Body and Sword

Looming over your opponent with your body in an aggressive attitude and your sword in a passive attitude, you draw out a first move from your opponent by means of your body, feet, or hands, you gain victory by inducing your opponent to take the initiative. Thus, your body and feet are in the aggressive mode, while your sword is in the passive mode. The purpose of putting your body and feet in the aggressive mode is to get your opponent to make the first move.

Mental and Physical Aggressive and Passive Modes

The mind should be in the passive mode, the body in the aggressive mode. The reason for this is that if the mind is in the aggressive mode, you will rush, and that is wrong. Therefore you control the mind and keep it impassive while using physical aggressiveness to get the opponent to make the first move, and thus you gain victory. If the mind is aggressive, you will lose by trying to kill your opponent right away.

In another sense, it can be understood that the mind is to be in the aggressive mode and the body in the passive mode. The point of this is to cause your mind to work intently, putting the mind in an aggressive mode while keeping your sword passive, getting your adversary to make the first move.

The "body" can be understood to mean the hands that hold the sword. Thus it is said that the mind is aggressive while the body is passive.

Although there are two meanings, ultimately the sense is the same. In any case, you win by inducing your opponent to take the initiative.

Things to Learn When You Face an Aggressive Opponent

There are three points on which to focus the eyes: (1) the Two Stars (the opponent's two hands gripping his sword); (2) Peak and Valley (the bending and extension of the opponent's arms); and (3) when engaged, the Distant Mountains (the shoulders and chest). The details of these points of eye focus are to be transmitted orally.

The next two items have to do with the sword and the posture of the body: (1) the rhythm of the distance and (2) the position of the body and the sandalwood state of mind.

The next five items are in the body and in the sword; they are impossible to explain in writing, and each one must be learned by dueling: (1) making the fist into a shield; (2) making the body unified; (3) taking an opponent's fist on your shoulder; (4) the sense of extending the rear leg; and (5) adopting the same stance and guard as the opponent, whatever it may be.

Anyway, the proper state of mind in all five items is to prepare yourself carefully before facing off with an opponent, not allowing yourself to be inattentive; it is essential to make sure that you do not get shook up once the duel begins. If you face off suddenly, without mental preparation, the moves you have learned will not be forthcoming.

Things Learned for Facing Off in a Contest of Adversaries

As for the significance of these three items—the Two Stars, Peak and Valley, and the Distant Mountains—when an opponent is firmly entrenched in a passive, waiting mode, you should not take your eyes off the places described in these three expressions.

These points of focus, however, are used for both aggressive and passive modes. These points of focus are essential. When wading in slashing, you focus your eyes on the Peak. When exchanging blows, you focus your eyes on the Distant Mountains. As for the Two Stars, you should always keep an eye on them.

The Mental Postures of Three Ways of Feinting

The three ways of feinting are three ways of seeing: sticking, pinning, and studied assault. When you cannot tell what opponents might do, you should use these three feints to feel them out.

The thing is to find out adversaries' intentions. When opponents are secured in a passive or waiting mode, you cast these three kinds of impression for the three ways of seeing, implementing strategic maneuvers with covert intentions, inducing adversaries to tip their hands, and thus using this to enable you to gain victory.

ADDRESSING AND ADAPTING TO CHANGES OF MIND

The sense of this is that when you deliberately convey various changes of mind to passive opponents, their changes of mind become evident. You win by adapting to those changes of mind.

DOUBLE LOOKS

When you try various ploys on passive opponents to see what they will do, you see without looking, seeing without appearing to see, constantly attentive, not placing your eyes on one single place, you shift your eyes around, seeing in quick glances.

There is a line of a poem that says, "Watching in stolen glances, the dragonfly evades the shrike." Seeing a shrike in a stolen glance, a dragonfly takes to flight. Quickly but surely seeing the actions of opponents in stolen glances, you should work with constant attention.

In *Nōh* drama, there is something called the double look. This means to look and see, then shift the eyes to the side. This means not fixing the gaze.

Hit and Be Hit At: The Sense of Winning by Letting Yourself Be Hit At

It is easy to kill someone with a slash of a sword. It is hard to be impossible for others to cut down.

Even if someone lashes out at you with the intention of cutting you down, carefully note the margin of safety where you are out of reach, and calmly let yourself be hit at by the enemy. Even if an adversary lashes out thinking he will score a blow, as long as there is that margin, he will not manage to strike you.

A stroke of the sword that does not hit its target is the sword stroke of death; you reach over it to strike the winning blow. Your adversary's initiative having missed its mark, you turn the tables around and get the jump on your adversary.

Once a sword fight has started, the thing is not to let your opponent raise his hands. Once the fight has started, if you get involved in thinking about what to do, you will be cut down by your opponent with the very next sword blow.

Here you will lose if you are inattentive. You get hit by your opponent when your mind dallies on the blow you have just struck, making naught of your initiative. When you strike a blow, do not let your mind dally on it, not concerning yourself with whether or not it is a telling blow; you should strike again and again, over and over, even four and five times. The thing is not to let the opponent even raise his head.

As for victory, it is determined by a single blow of the sword.

Three Rhythms

One rhythm is a simultaneous strike. Another is to close in and strike when the adversary's sword is raised. The third is to cross over and strike when the adversary's sword is lowered.

Matching rhythm is bad, incongruous rhythm is good. If your rhythm matches, that makes it easier for an adversary to use his sword. If your rhythm is incongruous, the adversary's sword is rendered useless.

You should strike in such a way as to make it difficult for opponents to use their swords. Whether closing in or crossing over, you should strike unrhythmically. In general and in particular, a rhythm that can be tapped into is bad.

A Small Rhythm to a Large Rhythm, a Large Rhythm to a Small Rhythm

When an adversary wields his sword in a large rhythm, you should use yours with a small rhythm. If your adversary uses a small rhythm, you should use a large rhythm. Here, too, the idea is to use your sword in such a way that the rhythm is incongruous with that of your opponent. If he gets into your rhythm, the adversary's sword becomes easy to employ.

For example, since an expert song goes over the intervals without lapsing into a fixed pattern, a mediocre drummer cannot drum to it. Just as if you put a mediocre drummer in with an expert singer, or a mediocre singer in with an expert drummer, making it hard to sing and drum, to contrive in such a way to make it impossible for opponents to strike, is called "a small rhythm to a large rhythm, a large rhythm to a small rhythm."

Even if a mediocre singer tries to handle a grandiose rhythm fluently, or an expert drummer tries to tap a little rhythm lightly, it will not work. Also, if an expert singer sings lightly, a mediocre drummer will fall behind and be unable to keep time.

An expert bird hunter shows the bird his pole, shaking it to make it jiggle, smoothly using that as a means to spear the prey. The bird, mesmerized by the rhythm of the jiggling pole, flaps its wings trying to take off but is unable to take off and thus gets speared.

It is imperative to act in a rhythm different from that of adversaries. If your rhythm is incongruous, you can wade right in without your own defenses being crossed. Such a state of mind should also be savored as an object of reflective study.

Noting the Tempo

Neither song nor dance can be performed without knowing the tempo. There must also be a sense of tempo in martial arts. To see with certainty how an adversary's sword is working, how he is handling it, and to discern what is in his mind, must be the same state of mind as that of one who has mastered the tempos of song and dance. When you know your opponent's moves and manners well, you can make your own maneuvers freely.

TECHNIQUES I

1. Accompanying a blow of the sword
2. Three inches on either side, opposing or supporting
3. Sneaking in quickly
4. Focusing the eyes on the elbows in the upper position
5. Circling swords; keeping an eye on both right and left
6. Reckoning the three-foot margin

The above six items are learned by working with a teacher and must be taught by word of mouth. They are not completely revealed in writing.

When you use such techniques to launch various preliminary blows and project appearances with covert intentions, and yet your adversary remains unruffled and refuses to make a move, remaining secure in a passive waiting mode, when you then sneak into the range of the sword, slipping right up to your adversary, he can no longer hold back and shifts into the aggressive mode; then you induce the adversary to take the initiative, whereupon you let him hit out at you, and thus strike him down.

In any case, if the opponent does not lash out, you cannot win. Even if an opponent lashes out at you, if you have properly learned how to gauge the margin of safety where you are out of reach, you will not get struck all of a sudden. Having practiced this step thoroughly, you can fearlessly slip right up to an adversary, get him to lash out, and then turn the tables on him to win. This is the sense of being a step ahead of the one who takes the initiative.

Techniques II

1. The major opus, including the initial assault; this must be transmitted by word of mouth.
2. Sustained attention, used in both aggressive and passive modes; this must be transmitted by word of mouth.
3. The one-cubit margin of a small sword.
4. The existence of both aggressive and passive modes when attacking should be understood as the body being in the aggressive mode while the sword is passive.

Each of the above items is learned by working with a teacher and must be passed on by word of mouth. It is impossible to express them well in writing.

Hearing the Sound of Wind and Water

This science is in any case all about how to win by getting your opponent to take the initiative, using tactical ploys as your basis, launching various preliminary blows, and shifting strategically.

Before facing off, you should consider your adversary to be in the aggressive mode, and should not be inattentive. Mental preparation is essential. If you do not think of your adversary as in the aggressive mode, the techniques you have been learning all along will be of no avail once you are attacked with great vehemence the very instant the duel starts.

Once you have faced off, it is essential to put your mind, body, and feet in the aggressive mode, while putting your hands in the waiting mode. You should be sure to pay attention to what is there. This is what is meant by the saying "Take what is there in hand." If you do not observe with utmost calm, the sword techniques you have learned will not be useful.

As for the matter of "hearing the sound of wind and water," this means being calm and quiet above while keeping an aggressive mood underneath. Wind has no sound; it produces sound when it hits things. Thus wind is silent when it blows up above. When it makes contact with things like trees and bamboo below, the sound it produces is noisy and frantic.

Water also has no sound when it is falling from above; it makes a frantic sound down below when it comes down and hits things.

Using these images as illustrations, the point is to be calm and quiet above, while sustaining an aggressive mood underneath. These are images of being extremely serene, unruffled, and calm on the surface, while inwardly being aggressively watchful.

It is bad when the body, hands, and feet are hurried. The aggressive and passive modes should be paired, one inward and one outward; it is bad to settle into just one mode. It is imperative to reflect on the sense of yin and yang alternating. Movement is yang, stillness is yin. Yin and yang interchange, inside and outside. When yang moves inwardly, outwardly be still, in the yin mode; when you are inwardly yin, movement appears outwardly.

In this kind of martial art as well, inwardly you activate your mental energy, constantly attentive, while outwardly you remain unruffled and calm. This is yang moving within, while yin is quiet without. This is in accord with the pattern of nature.

Furthermore, when outwardly intensely aggressive, if you are calm within while aggressive without, so that your inner mind is not captured by the outside, then you will not be outwardly wild. If you move both inwardly and outwardly at once, you become wild. The aggressive and passive modes, movement and stillness, should be made to alternate inside and outside.

Keeping the inner mind attentive, like a duck swimming on the water, calm above while paddling below, when this practice builds up, the inner mind and the outside both melt, so that inside and outside become one, without the slightest obstruction. To reach this state is the supreme attainment.

Sickness

It is sickness to be obsessed with winning, it is sickness to be obsessed with using martial arts, and it is sickness to be obsessed with putting forth all one has learned. It is sickness to be obsessed with offense, and it is also sickness to be obsessed with defense. It is also sickness to be obsessed with getting rid of sickness. To fix the mind obsessively on anything is considered sickness. Since all of these various sicknesses are in the mind, the thing is to tune the mind by getting rid of such afflictions.

The Sense of Elementary and Advanced Levels of Removal of Sickness

The elementary level of removing sickness is when you get into thought to be free from thought and get into attachment to be free from attachment.

The meaning of this is that the wish to get rid of sickness is thought; to wish to get rid of the sicknesses in your mind is to be "in the midst of thought."

Also, even though we use the term sickness, this means obsessive thought. To think of getting rid of sickness is also thought. Therefore you use thought to get rid of thought. When you get rid of thoughts, you are free from thought, so this is called getting into thought to be free from thought.

When you take thought to get rid of the sickness that remains in thought, after that the thought of removal and the thoughts to be removed both disappear. This is what is known as using a wedge to extract a wedge.

When you cannot get a wedge out, if you drive another one in so as to ease the tightness, the first wedge comes out. Once the stuck wedge comes out, the wedge driven in afterward does not remain. When sickness is gone, the thought of getting rid of sickness no longer remains; so this is called getting into thought to be free from thought.

To think of getting rid of sickness is to be attached to sickness, but if you use that attachment to get rid of sickness, the attachment will not remain; so this is called getting into attachment to be free from attachment.

In the advanced level, getting rid of sickness means having no thought whatsoever of getting rid of sickness. To think of riddance is itself sickness. To let sickness be, while living in the midst of sickness, is to be rid of sickness.

Thinking of getting rid of sickness happens because sickness is still in the mind. Therefore sickness does not leave at all, and whatever you do and think is done with attachment; so there can be no higher value in it.

How is this to be understood? The two levels, elementary and advanced, have been set up for this function. You cultivate the state of mind of the elementary level, and when this cultivation builds up, attachment leaves on its own, without your intending to get rid of it.

Sickness means attachment. Attachment is despised in Buddhism. Mendicants who are free from attachment can mix in with the ordinary world without being affected or influenced; whatever they do is done freely and independently, stopping where it naturally should.

Masters of the arts cannot be called adepts as long as they have not left behind attachment to their various skills. Dust and dirt adhere to an unpolished gem, but a perfectly polished gem will not be dirtied even if it falls into mud. Polishing the gem of your mind by spiritual cultivation so that it is impervious to stain, leaving sickness alone and giving up concern, do as you will.

The Normal Mind

A monk asked an ancient worthy, "What is the Way?" He replied, "The normal mind is the Way."

The story contains a principle that applies to all the arts. Asked what the Way is, the ancient worthy replied that the normal mind is the Way. This is truly the ultimate. This is the state where the sicknesses of mind are all gone and one has become normal in mind, free from sickness even when in the midst of the sickness.

To apply this to worldly matters, suppose you are shooting with a bow and you think you are shooting while you are shooting; then the aim of your bow will be inconsistent and unsteady. When you wield a sword, if you are conscious of wielding a sword, your offense will be unstable. When you are writing, if you are conscious of writing, your pen will be unsteady. Even when you play the harp, if you are conscious of playing, the tune will be off.

When an archer forgets consciousness of shooting and shoots in a normal frame of mind, as if unoccupied, the bow will be steady. When using a sword or riding a horse as well, you do not "wield a sword" or "ride a horse." And you do not "write," you do not "play music." When you do everything in the normal state of mind, as it is when totally unoccupied, then everything goes smoothly and easily.

Whatever you do as your Way, if you are obsessed with it, or think that this alone is of importance to you, then it is not the Way. It is when you have nothing in your chest that you are on the Way. Whatever you do, if you do it with nothing in your chest, it works out easily.

This is like the way everything reflects clearly in a mirror precisely because of the formless clarity of the mirror's reflectiveness. The heart of those on the Way is like a mirror, empty and clear, being mindless and yet not failing to accomplish anything.

This is the "normal mind." Someone who does everything with this normal mind is called an adept.

Whatever you do, if you keep the idea of doing it before you and do it with singleminded concentration, you will be uncoordinated. You will do it well once, and then, when you think that is fine, you will do it badly. Or you may do it well twice, then do it badly again. If you are glad you did it well twice and badly only once, then you will do it badly again. There is no consistency at all, because of doing it with the thought of doing it well.

When the effects of exercise build up unawares and practice accumulates, thoughts of wishing to quickly develop skill disappear quietly, and whatever you do, you spontaneously become free from conscious thoughts. At this time, you do not even know yourself; when your body, feet, and hands act without your doing anything in your mind, you make no misses, ten times out of ten.

Even then, if it gets on your mind, you will miss. When you are not consciously mindful, you will succeed every time. Not being consciously mindful does not, however, mean total mindlessness; it just means a normal mind.

Like a Wooden Man Facing Flowers and Birds

This is a saying of Layman Pang: "Like a wooden man facing flowers and birds." Although his eyes are on the flowers and birds, his mind does not stir at the flowers and birds.

Because a wooden man has no mind, it is not moved; this is perfectly logical. But how does a person with a mind become like a wooden man?

The wooden man is a metaphor, an illustration. As a human being with a mind, one cannot be exactly like a wooden manikin. As a human being, one cannot be like bamboo and wood. Even though you do see flowers, you do not see them by reproducing the consciousness of seeing the flowers.

The point of the saying is just to see innocently with the normal mind. When you shoot, you do not shoot by reproducing the consciousness of shooting. In other words, you shoot with the normal mind.

The normal mind is called unminding. If you change the normal mind and instead reproduce another consciousness, your form will also change, so you will stir both internally and externally. If you do everything with a stirring mind, nothing will be as it should.

Even if it is only a matter of speaking a word, people will praise it if and only if your manner of saying it is unstirring and unshakable. What they call the unstirring mind of the Buddhas seems truly sublime.

THE FREE MIND

Master Zhongfeng said, "Embody the free-minded mind." There are elementary and advanced levels of applying this saying.

When you let the mind go, it stops where it has gone; therefore the first level of practice is to get it to come back each time, so that the mind does not stay anywhere. When you strike a blow of the sword and your mind lingers where you struck, this teaching has you get it to return to you.

At the advanced level, the message is to let your mind be free to go wherever it will. You release your mind after having made it such that it will not stop and linger anywhere even if it is set free.

To embody the free-minded mind means that as long as you use the mind that releases the mind to rope the mind and keep dragging it back, you are not free and independent. The mind that does not stop and linger anywhere even when it is set free is called the free-minded mind.

When you embody this free-minded mind, you can act independently. You are not independent as long as you are holding on to a halter. Even dogs and cats should be raised unleashed. Cats and dogs cannot be raised properly if they are tied up all the time.

People who read Confucian books dwell on the word *seriousness* as if it were the ultimate, spending their whole lives on seriousness, thus making their minds like leashed cats.

In Buddhism as well, seriousness does in fact exist. Scripture speaks of being singleminded and undistracted. This would correspond to seriousness. It means to place the mind on one thing and not scatter it elsewhere.

There are, of course, passages that say, "We seriously declare of the Buddha . . . ," and we speak of singlemindedly and seriously paying respects when we face a Buddha image in what we call reverent obeisance. These usages all have meanings congruous with that of seriousness.

However, these are in any case expedient means for quelling distraction of mind. A well-governed mind does not use expedients to pacify it.

When we chant "Great Sage, Immovable One," with our posture correct and our hands joined in a gesture of reverence, in our minds we visualize the image of the Immovable One. At this time, our three modes of action, physical, verbal, and mental, are equal, and we are singleminded and undistracted. This is called "equality of the three mysteries." In other words, this has the same import as seriousness.

Seriousness corresponds to a quality of the basic mind, yet it is a state of mind that lasts only so long as it is practiced. When we let go of our reverential gesture and stop chanting Buddha names, the image of Buddha in our minds also disappears. What then remains is the former distracted mind. This is not a thoroughly pacified mind.

People who have successfully managed to pacify their minds once do not purify their physical, verbal, and mental actions; they are unstained even as they mingle with the dust of the world. Even if they are active all day, they are unmoved, just as the moon reflected in the water does not move even though thousands and tens of thousands of waves roll one after another. This is the state of people who have consummated Buddhism; I have recorded it here under the instruction of a teacher of that doctrine.

THE LIFE-GIVING SWORD

PERCEIVING ABILITIES AND INTENTIONS

There may be a hundred stances and sword positions,
but you win with just one." The ultimate point of this
is perceiving abilities and intentions.

Even if a hundred or a thousand manners of swordplay are taught and learned, including all sorts of
positions of the body and the sword, the perception of
abilities and intentions alone is to be considered the eye.

Even if your opponent knows a hundred stances and
you know a hundred stances, the ultimate point is solely
in the perception of abilities and intentions.

Because this is transmitted secretly, it is not written
in the real way, but in homophonic code words.

THE RHYTHM OF EXISTENCE AND NONEXISTENCE

And the Existence of Both the Existent and the Nonexistent

These expressions refer to the custom of using the
terms existence and nonexistence in reference to abilities and intentions. When evident, they are existent,

when concealed, they are nonexistent. These hiding and revealing "existence and nonexistence" refers to perceptions of abilities and intentions. They are in the hand that grips the sword.

There are analyses of existence and nonexistence in Buddhism; here we use these terms analogously. Ordinary people see the existent, but not the nonexistent. In perception of abilities and intentions, we see both the existent and the nonexistent.

The fact is that existence and nonexistence are both there. When there is existence, you strike the existent; when there is nonexistence, you strike the nonexistent. Also, you strike the nonexistent without waiting for its existence, and strike the existent without waiting for its nonexistence. Therefore it is said that both existence and nonexistence are there.

In a commentary on the classic of Lao-tzu, there is something called "always existent, always nonexistent." Existence is always there, and nonexistence is always there as well. When concealed, existence becomes nonexistence; when revealed, nonexistence becomes existence.

For example, when a duck is floating on top of the water, it is "present," and when it dives under the water, it is "absent." So even when we think something exists, once it is concealed it is nonexistent. And even if we think something is nonexistent, when it is revealed it exists. Therefore existence and nonexistence just mean concealment and manifestation, of what is essentially the same thing. Thus existence and nonexistence are both always there.

In Buddhism, they speak of fundamental nonexistence and fundamental existence. When people die, the existent is concealed. When people are born, the nonexistent is manifested. The reality is the same thing.

There are existence and nonexistence in the hand that grips the sword. This is transmitted secretly. This is called perception of ability and intention. When you have hidden your hand, what you have there is concealed. When you turn your palm face up, what is not there is revealed.

Even so, without personal transmission, these words are hard to understand.

When there is existence, you should see this existence and strike it. When there is nonexistence, you should see this nonexistence and strike it. That is why we say that both existence and nonexistence exist.

The thing called existence is nonexistent. The thing called nonexistence exists. Existence and nonexistence are not two.

If you misperceive the existence and nonexistence of abilities and intentions, even if you use a hundred techniques to the fullest, you will not attain victory. Every sort of martial art is consummated in this one step.

The Moon in the Water And Its Reflection

There is a certain distance between an adversary and yourself at which you will not get hit by the adversary's sword. You employ martial arts from outside this space.

To get close to an opponent by striding into this space or slipping into it is called "the moon in the water," being likened to the moon sending its reflection into a body of water.

One should engage an opponent only after having set up a theoretical "moon in the water" field in one's mind before even facing off. The measurement of the spacing has to be transmitted by word of mouth.

The Quiescent Sword

The quiescent sword is a most extremely important matter. There is in oneself a way to wear it as a quiet sword; in reference to oneself, the character for *sword* (*ken*) in "quiescent sword" is written and understood as "sword." Whether it is positioned to the right or the left, as long as the sword has not left the state of quiescence, there is meaning in the use of the character for *sword*.

Then again, in reference to adversaries, the character *ken* for "sword" should be written and understood as the word *ken* for "see." Since you are to see the position of quiescent swords clearly in order to wade in slashing, the seeing is essential. Thus there is meaning in the character *ken* for "seeing."

EXPLANATION OF THE CHARACTERS USED FOR "QUIESCENT"

[The two characters used for "quiescent" in the expression "quiescent sword" literally mean "spirit" and "wonder."] The spirit is within, the wonder manifests outwardly; this is called an inscrutable marvel. For example, because there is the spirit of tree within a tree, therefore its flowers blossom fragrantly, it turns green, its branches and leaves flourish; this is called the marvel.

Even though you may break wood down, you do not see anything you may call the spirit of tree; yet if there were no spirit, the flowers and foliage would not come out. This is also true of the human spirit; even though you cannot open up the body to see something you may call the spirit, it is by virtue of the existence of the spirit within that you perform various actions.

When you stabilize the spirit in situations where swords are quiescent, thereby all sorts of marvels appear in the hands and feet, causing flowers to bloom in battle.

The spirit is the master of the mind. The spirit resides within, employing the mind outside. This mind, furthermore, employs psychic energy. Employing psychic energy in external activities for the sake of the spirit, if this mind lingers in one place, its function is deficient. Therefore it is essential to make sure that the mind is not fixated on one point.

For example, when the master of a house, staying at home, sends a servant out on an errand, if the servant stays where he goes and does not return, he will be missing for further service. In the same way, if your mind lingers on things and does not return to its original state, your ability in martial arts will slip.

For this reason, the matter of not fixating the mind on one point applies to everything, not only martial arts.

There are two understandings, spirit and mind.

STRIDE

Your stride should not be too quick or too slow. Steps should be taken in an unruffled, casual manner.

It is bad to go too far or not far enough; take the mean. When you go too quickly, it means you are scared and flustered. When you go too slowly, it means you are timid and frightened.

The desired state is one in which you are not upset at all.

Usually people will blink when something brushes by right in front of their eyes. This is normal, and the fact that you blink your eyes does not mean that you are upset. Also, if something is swung at your eyes two or three more times to startle you, if you did not blink your eyes at all, that would actually mean you were upset.

To deliberately hold back spontaneous blinking indicates a much more disturbed mind than does blinking.

The immovable or imperturbable mind is normal. If something comes at your eyes, you blink. This is the state of not being upset. The essential point is just not losing the normal state of mind. To try not to move is to have moved. To move is an immovable principle.

It is good to take steps in a normal manner, and in a normal frame of mind. This is the stage where neither your appearance nor your mind is upset.

THE FIRST PRINCIPLE
The Mental Attitude in a Faceoff Is as When Facing a Spear. What to Do When You Have No Sword.

"The first principle" is a code word in martial arts. In the context of the art of war in general, it means to be independent in every possible way.

The important thing is what happens when you are hard pressed. "The first principle" means you keep that clearly in mind, pay close attention, and make sure you do not get caught in a pinch, unprepared.

The concentrated attention exerted in a face-to-face confrontation with swords when an opponent's stab nearly reaches you, or when a spear is thrust into the cubit margin of safety, is called the first principle.

This is the concentrated attention exerted at such times as when you are being attacked with your back to a wall. It should be understood as a most critical and most difficult situation.

When you have no sword, the one-cubit margin of safety is quite impossible to maintain if you fix your eyes on one spot, let your mind linger on one place, and fail to keep up sustained watchfulness.

To keep things like this in mind is called the first principle, something that is kept secret.

THE ONE-FOOT MARGIN ON BOTH SIDES
When Both Swords Are the Same Size, Attention Is to Be Concentrated in the Same Way as When Having No Sword.

The weapons on both sides are one foot away from the body. With a margin of one foot, you can slip and parry. It is dangerous to get within this space.

"THIS IS THE ULTIMATE"/THE FIRST SWORD

"This is the ultimate" is a manner of referring to what is supremely consummate. "The first sword" does not literally refer to a sword. "The first sword" is a code word for seeing incipient movement on the part of opponents. The expression "the critical first sword" means that seeing what opponents are trying to do is the first sword in the ultimate sense.

Understanding the perception of impulses and incipient actions of adversaries as the first sword, understand the weapon that strikes according to what they do as the second sword.

With this as fundamental, you use it in various ways. Perceiving abilities and intentions, the moon in the water, the quiescent sword, and sicknesses make four; with the working of hands and feet, all together they make five. These are learned as "five observations, one seeing."

To perceive abilities and intentions is called "one seeing." The other four are held in mind, so they are called observations. Perceiving with the eyes is called seeing, perceiving with the mind is called observation. This means contemplation in the mind.

The reason we do not call this four observations and one seeing, instead speaking of five observations, is that we use five observations as an inclusive term, of which one, perceiving abilities and intentions, is called "one seeing."

Perceiving abilities and intentions; the moon in the water; the quiescent sword; sickness; body, hands, and feet: these are five items. Four of these are observed in the mind, while the perception of abilities and intentions is seen with the eyes and is called "one seeing."

ANALYSIS OF THE MOON IN THE WATER; THE QUIESCENT SWORD; SICKNESS; BODY, HANDS, AND FEET

The moon in the water is a matter of the choice of the physical setting of a duel. The quiescent sword is a matter of the choice of your own location. Body, hands, and feet refer to watching what opponents do, and to your own movements. Getting rid of sickness is for the purpose of perceiving abilities and intentions. Therefore the primary thing is to perceive the existence or nonexistence of abilities and intentions. The other four are generalities.

Getting rid of sickness is for the purpose of seeing abilities and intentions. As long as you are not rid of sickness, you will be distracted by it and fail to see. When you fail to see, you lose.

Sickness means sickness of mind. Sickness of mind is when the mind tarries here and there. One should make sure not to let the mind linger on the point where one has struck a blow of the sword. This is a matter of relinquishing the mind without abandoning it.

Moves

If an adversary is positioned such that the tip of his sword is facing you, strike as he raises it. When you intend to strike an opponent, let him hit at you. As long as your adversary lashes out at you, you have as good as struck him.

The Margin of Safety

Take up a position at the margin of safety; after that, concentrate on your state of mind.

When you try to take up a position, if your adversary has already taken up a position, make that yours.

As long as the spacing does not change, even if your opponent approaches five feet, or you approach five feet, the distance between you and your opponent remains the same.

If others have taken up positions, it is best to let them take those positions for the time being. It is bad to get too wrapped up in jockeying for position. Keep your body buoyant.

Maneuvering

Footwork and disposition of the body should be such as not to miss the location of the quiescent sword. This determination should be remembered all along, from even before facing off.

Seeing the Quiescent Sword: Distinction of Three Levels

Seeing with the mind is considered basic. It is because of seeing from the mind that the eyes also perceive. Therefore seeing with the eyes is subordinate to seeing with the mind. Next after that is to see with your body, feet, and hands.

Seeing with your body, feet, and hands means that you do not let your body, feet, and hands miss the quiescent sword of an adversary. Seeing with the mind is for the purpose of seeing with the eyes. Seeing with the eyes means aiming your feet and hands at the location of an adversary's quiescent sword.

"The Mind Is Like the Moon in Water, the Body Is Like an Image in a Mirror."

The sense in which these expressions are applied to martial arts is as follows.

Water reflects an image of the moon, a mirror reflects an image of a person's body. The reflection of things in the human mind is like the reflection of the moon in the water, reflecting instantaneously.

The location of the quiescent sword is likened to water, your mind is likened to the moon. The mind should be reflected in the location of the quiescent sword. Where the mind goes, the body goes; the body follows the mind.

A mirror is also likened to the quiescent sword, in which case these expressions are used to mean moving your body to the locus of the quiescent sword like a reflection. The principle is not letting your hands and feet miss the location of the quiescent sword.

The reflecting of the moon in the water is an instantaneous phenomenon. Even though it is way out in space, the moon casts its reflection in water the very instant the clouds disappear. The reflection does not descend gradually from the sky; it is cast at once, before you can even blink an eye. This is a simile for the way things reflect in people's minds as immediately as the moon reflects in a body of water.

There is a passage of Buddhist scripture that says the mind is as instantaneous as the moon reflected in water or an image cast in a mirror. The point of this is not that the moon reflected in water appears to be there but is not. It simply refers to casting an instant reflection from far away in the sky. A form being reflected in a mirror, which immediately reflects whatever is before it, is also a simile for immediacy.

This is the way the human mind reflects in things. The mind may travel even as far as China in the blink of an eye. Just as you think you are dozing off, your dreams travel to your native village far away. The Buddha explained this kind of reflection of the mind as being like the moon in water or images in a mirror.

These expressions also apply similarly to "the moon in the water" in martial arts. You should transfer your mind to the appropriate locus like the moon reflecting in a body of water. Where the mind goes, the body goes; so as soon as a face-off begins, you should shift your body to the appropriate spot like an image reflecting in a mirror. If you do not send your mind there beforehand in preparation, your body will not go.

In reference to the locus, it is "the moon in the water." In terms of the person, it is "the quiescent sword." In either case, the sense of shifting the body, feet, and hands is the same.

Hasty Attack

A hasty attack is an exceptionally bad thing. The thing is to press aggressively only after having properly prepared yourself mentally and having observed the situation thoroughly once the face-off has begun. It is essential not to get flustered.

Bringing Back the Mind

The sense of this expression is that when you strike a blow of the sword, if you think to yourself that you have scored, then the mind thinking you have scored stops and stays right there. Since your mind does not come back from the blow you have scored, you become careless and get hit by the adversary's "second sword." Your initiative turns out to be for naught, and you lose by getting hit with a counterblow.

When you strike a blow, do not keep your mind on where you hit; after striking, bring your mind back to observe your adversary's condition. Once he is struck, an opponent's mood changes; when one gets hit, one becomes resentful and angry. When angered, an adversary becomes vehement; if you are inattentive, you will get hit.

Think of an adversary who has been hit as a raging wild boar. When you are conscious of having struck a blow, you let your mind tarry and are thus inattentive. You should be aware that an opponent's energy will emerge when he is hit. Also, an adversary will be careful of a place where he has already been hit, so if you try to strike again in the same way, you will miss. When you miss, your opponent will counter and hit you.

Bringing back the mind means bringing your mind back to your body, not letting it tarry at the point where you have struck. The thing is to bring your mind back to observe your opponent's condition.

On the other hand, to repeatedly strike when you have struck a focused blow, slashing again and again without bringing your mind back, not letting your opponent so much as turn his head, this too is a supremely effective state of mind. This is what is meant by the expression "not a hairsbreadth's gap." The idea is to keep slashing without the slightest interval between one stroke and the next.

In a Zen dialogue, which is referred to as a religious battlefield, an answer is given to a question without the slightest gap. If you delay, you will be overtaken by your opponent. Then it is clear who will win and who will lose.

This is what is meant by leaving no gap, not even so much as could admit a single strand of hair. It refers to rapidity of the sword in repeated strokes.

The Sense of Total Removal, the Sense of the Void, the Sense of Presenting the Mind

Total removal means completely removing all sickness. Sickness here means sickness of mind. The thing is to get rid of all the sickness in the mind in one fell swoop.

The varieties of sickness are indicated elsewhere in this book. The general meaning of sickness is the lingering or tarrying of the mind. In Buddhism this is called clinging, and it is severely rejected. If the mind clings to one spot and lingers there, you will miss what you should see, and suffer unexpected defeat.

The expression "total removal" refers to the idea that one should get rid of all these sicknesses in one fell swoop. The sense is that one should totally remove all sicknesses and not fail to perceive "the only one."

Now then, "the only one" refers to the void. "The void" is a code word, which has to be taught secretly. It refers to the mind of an adversary. Mind is shapeless and immaterial; that is why it is "void." To see "the void, the only one" means to see the minds of adversaries.

Buddhism is a matter of realizing the emptiness of mind. Although there are people who preach that mind is empty, it is said that there are few who realize it.

As for "presenting the mind," the mind of an adversary is presented in the hands that grip the sword. The thing is to strike the adversary's grip before he even makes a move.

"Complete removal" is for the purpose of seeing that moment of imminent movement. The point is to get rid of all sicknesses at once, and not fail to see "the void."

The mind of an adversary is in his hands; it is presented in his hands. To hit them while they are still is called hitting the void. The void does not move, has no form, no motion. To hit the void means swiftly striking before movement.

Voidness is the eye of Buddhism. There is a distinction between false voidness and real voidness. False voidness is a simile for nothingness. Real voidness is genuine emptiness, which is the emptiness of mind. Although the mind is like empty space insofar as it is formless, the one mind is the master of the body, so the performance of all actions is in the mind.

The movement and working of the mind is the doing of the mind. When the mind is inactive, it is void; when the void is active, it is mind. The void goes into motion, becoming mind and working in the hands and feet. Since you are to hit the adversary's hands holding the sword quickly, before they move, it is said that you should "hit the void."

Even though we speak of "presenting the mind," the mind is invisible to the eye. It is called void because of being invisible, and it is also called void when it is not moving. Although the mind is presented in the hands gripping a sword, it is invisible to the eye. The point is to strike when the mind is presented in the hands but has not yet moved.

If you suppose that this mind-void is nothing because it is invisible, yet when the mind-void moves, it does all sorts of things. Gripping with the hands, treading with the feet, all possible marvels are products of the action of this void, this mind.

It is hard to understand this mind by reading books; this is a path hard to reach by listening to sermons. People who write and people who preach just write and preach based on traditional religious writings and lectures; those who have realized the mind at heart are rare.

Since all human actions, even marvels, are doings of the mind, this mind is also in the universe. We call this the mind of the universe. When this mind moves, there is thunder and lightning, wind and rain; it does things like create unseasonable cloud formations and cause hail to rain in midsummer, producing ill effects on humanity.

Thus, in the context of the universe, the void is the master of the universe; and in the context of the human body, it is the master of the human body. When dancing, it is the master of dance; when acting, it is the master of drama. When shooting, it is the master of the gun and bow; when riding, it is the master of the horse.

If there is a personal warp in the master, one cannot ride a horse or hit the mark with a bow or a gun.

When the mind has found its proper place and position in the body and is settled where it ought to be, one is free in all paths. It is important to find this mind and understand it.

People all think they have perceived and opened up their own minds and are able to employ their own minds usefully, but very few people have actually found this mind for sure. The signs that they have not attained realization will be evident in their persons, visible to all who have the perception to see.

When people are awakened, everything they do, all their physical actions, will be direct. If they are not upright, they can hardly be called enlightened people. The direct, upright mind is called the original mind, or the mind of the Way. The warped, polluted mind is called the false or errant mind, or the human mentality.

People who have actually realized their own original mind, and whose actions accord with that original mind, are a fascinating phenomenon. I do not speak such words from my own understanding. Although I speak like this, it is hard for me to be direct and straightforward in mind, and to behave in a manner consistent with a direct mind; nevertheless, I write of it because it is the Way.

Even so, in martial arts, technique cannot be perfected as long as your mind is not straight and your body, hands, and feet are not in accord. Although our everyday behavior is not in accord with the Way, in the path of martial arts this attainment of the Way is imperative.

Even though your actions are not apart from this mind, and you accord with this mind in a particular art, it does not work when you try to apply it elsewhere. One who knows everything and can do everything is called an adept. Those who master one art or one craft are called masters of their particular way, but this is not to be called adepthood.

True and False Mind

There is a poem that says,

> *It is the mind*
> *that is the mind*
> *confusing the mind.*
> *Do not leave the mind,*
> *O mind,*
> *to the mind.*

The mind in the first line refers to the false mind, which is bad because it is false and which confuses the original mind. The mind in the second line refers to the false mind. The mind in the third line refers to the original mind, which the false mind confuses. The mind in the fourth line refers to the original mind. The mind in the fifth line refers to the original mind. The mind in the sixth line refers to the false mind.

This poem expresses the true and the false. There are two minds, the original mind and the false mind. If you find the original mind and act in accord, all things are straightforward. When this original mind is warped and polluted by the obscurity of the false mind covering it up, all actions are therefore warped and polluted.

The original mind and the false mind are not two distinct entities. The original mind is the "original countenance," which is there before our parents give birth to us; having no form, it has no origination and no extinction. It is the physical body that is borne by our parents; since the mind is formless and immaterial, we cannot say our parents have given birth to it. It is inherently there in the body when people are born.

Zen is understood to be a teaching that communicates this mind. There is also imitation Zen. A lot of people say similar things that are not really the right path, so people who are supposedly Zennists are not all the same.

When we speak of the false mind, this refers to the energy of the blood, which is personal and subjective. Blood energy is the action of blood; when blood rises, the color of the face changes and one becomes angry.

Also, when people despise what we love, we become angry and resentful. But if others similarly despise what we despise, we enjoy this and twist wrong into right.

When people are given valuables, they receive them with delight; they break into smiles, and blood energy produces a glow in their faces. Then they take what is wrong to be right.

These are all states of mind that come from the energy in the blood in the body, from this physical body, when dealing with temporal situations. These states of mind are referred to as the false mind.

When this false mind is aroused, the original mind is concealed, becoming a false mind, so nothing but bad things emerge. Therefore enlightened people are honorable because they reduce the false mind by means of the original mind. In unenlightened people, the original mind is hidden, while the false mind is powerful; therefore they act wrongly and get a sullied reputation.

Although the poem quoted above is nothing special, it expresses the distinction between the false and true quite well. Whatever the false mind does is wrong. If this wrong mind emerges, you will lose at martial arts; you will miss the mark with bow and gun, and will not even be able to ride a horse. If you performed in a drama or a dance in this state, it would also be unpleasant to watch and listen. Mistakes will also show up in what you say. Everything will be off. If you accord with the original mind, however, everything you do will be good.

People contrive falsehoods, yet claim they are not false. That is the false mind acting, so its falsehood is immediately evident. If the heart is truthful, people who listen eventually realize it, without any need for explanations or rationalizations. The original mind needs no rationalizations or excuses.

The false mind is sickness of mind; getting rid of this false mind is called getting rid of sickness. Rid of this sickness, the mind is healthy. This sound mind is called the original mind. If you accord with the original mind, you will excel in martial arts. This principle is relevant to everything, without exception.

NO SWORD

Being "swordless" does not necessarily mean you have to take your opponent's sword. It also does not mean making a show of sword-snatching for your reputation. It is the swordless art of not getting killed when you have no sword. The basic intention is nothing like deliberately setting out to snatch a sword.

It is not a matter of insistently trying to wrest away what is being deliberately kept from your grasp. Not grasping attempts to avoid having it taken away is also "swordlessness." Someone who is intent upon not having his sword taken away forgets what he is opposed to and just tries to avoid having his sword taken away. Therefore he will be unable to kill anyone. Not being killed oneself is considered victory.

The principle is not to make an art of taking people's swords. It is learning to avoid being cut down by others when you have no sword yourself.

Swordlessness is not the art of taking another's sword. It is for the purpose of using all implements freely. When you are unarmed, if you can even take away another's sword and make it your own, then what will not be useful in your hands? Even if you only have a folding fan, you can still prevail over someone with a sword. This is the aim of swordlessness.

Suppose you are walking along with a bamboo cane, and someone draws a long sword and attacks you. You win if you take his sword away, even though you respond with only a cane; or if you do not take the sword away, you win if you thwart him so he cannot cut you down. This attitude should be regarded as the basic idea of swordlessness.

Swordlessness is not for the purpose of taking swords, nor for killing people. When an enemy insistently tries to kill you, that is when you should take his sword. The taking itself is not the original intention to start with. It is for the purpose of attaining an effective understanding of the margin of safety. This means gauging the distance between you and an enemy at which his sword will not hit you.

If you know the distance at which you are out of range, you are not fearful of an opponent's striking sword. When your body is exposed to attack, then you actively think about this exposure. When you have no sword, as long as you are out of range of another's sword, you cannot take it away. You have to be within striking range to take a sword; you have to expose yourself to being killed in order to take a sword away.

Swordlessness is the attitude whereby you let others have the swords, while you engage them using your hands as your instruments. So, since swords are longer than hands, you have to get close to an adversary, within killing range, in order to be successful at this.

It is necessary to distinguish the interplay of your opponent's sword and your hands. Then your adversary's sword overshoots your body, while you get underneath the hilt of the sword, aiming to arrest the sword. When the time comes, do not freeze into a fixed pattern. In any event, you cannot take away an opponent's sword unless you get right up close to him.

Swordlessness is the foremost secret of this school. Physical posture, positioning of the sword, taking a stand, distance, movement, contrivance, sticking, attacking, appearance and intention—all come from the attitude of swordlessness, so this is the essential eye.

Great Potential and Great Function

Everything has body and function. For example, a bow is a body, while drawing, shooting, and hitting the mark are functions of a bow. A lamp is a body, light is its function. Water is a body, moisture is a function of water. An apricot tree is a body, fragrance and color are functions. A sword is a body, cutting and stabbing are functions.

Therefore, potential is the body, while the existence of various capabilities, manifesting outwardly from the potential, is called function. Because an apricot tree has a body, flowers blossom from the body, giving off color and scent. In the same way, function resides within potential and works outside; sticking, attacking, appearance and intention, aggressive and passive modes, the casting of various impressions, and so on, manifest external action because there is potential at the ready within. These are called function.

Great is a word of praise. When we say "Great Spirit," "Great Incarnation," and "Great Saint," the word great is an expression of praise. Great function appears because of great potential. When Zen monks are able to use their bodies freely and independently, harmonizing with truth and communing with truth whatever they say and do, this is called "great spiritual power" or "great function of great potential."

Spiritual powers and miraculous manifestation are not wonders produced by ghosts or spirits from outer space; these terms refer to working freely and independently whatever you do. All the many sword positions, appearances concealing intentions, deceptions, use of implements, leaping up and leaping down, grabbing a blade, kicking someone down, all sorts of actions, are called great function when you attain independence, beyond what you have learned. Unless you always have the potential within, the great function will not appear.

Even when you are sitting indoors, first look up, then look left and right, to see if there is anything that might happen to fall from above. When you are seated by a door or a panel, take note of whether it might not fall over. If you happen to be in attendance near nobles of high rank, be aware of whether something unexpected might happen. Even when you are going in and out of a door, do not neglect attention to the going out and going in, always keeping aware.

All of these are examples of potential. When marvels come forth immediately at naturally appropriate times because the potential is always there within, this is called great function.

When the potential is unripe, however, the function does not manifest. In all paths, when concentration builds up and exercise is repeated, potential matures and great function emerges. When potential freezes, stiffens up, and remains inflexible, it is not functional. When it matures, it expands throughout the body, so that great function emerges through the hands and feet, eyes and ears.

When you meet people with this great potential and great function, martial arts using only what you have learned will not even enable you to raise a hand. Glared at once by the eyes of someone with the great potential, you will be so captivated by the look that you will forget to draw your sword, just standing there doing nothing.

If you delay for even the time it takes to blink an eye, you will have lost already. When a cat glares at it, a mouse falls down from the ceiling; captivated by the look in the cat's eyes, the mouse forgets even to run, and falls. Encountering someone with the great potential is like a mouse running into a cat.

There is a Zen saying that goes, "When the great function appears, it does not keep to guidelines." This means that people with the great potential and great function are not at all constrained by learning or rules. In all fields of endeavor, there are things to learn and there are rules. People who have attained supreme mastery are beyond them; they act freely and independently. To act independently, outside of rules, is called personifying great potential and great function.

Potential means to be thinking attentively of everything. Therefore, when that intently thought potential becomes stiff and frozen and hard, then you are entangled by potential and thus are not free. This is because potential is immature, unripe. If you build up effective exercise, potential will mature, expanding throughout the body, working freely and independently. This is called the great function.

Potential is mental energy. It is called potential according to the situation. Mind is the inside, mental energy is the entrance. Since the mind is the master of the whole body, it should be understood as that which resides within. Mental energy is at the door, working outside for its master, the mind.

The division of the mind into good and bad comes from potential, as it goes out from states of potential to good and to bad. Mental energy that is kept watchfully at the door is called potential. When people open a door and go outside, whether they do good, do evil, or even work marvels is due to the ideas in their minds before opening the door.

Thus this potential is something very important. If this potential is working, it emerges outside and the great function manifests. In any case, if you understand it as mental energy, you will not be off. It is called differently according to where it is.

Even so, just because we speak of the inside and the entrance, there are no fixed definitions of inside and entrance somewhere in the body. We speak of inside and entrance by way of metaphor. For example, when people speak, the beginning of their speech could be called the entrance, while the end could be called the inside; in the words themselves there are no specific locations of inside and entrance.

Mind and Objects

A verse of Saint Manora says, "Mind turns along with myriad situations; its turning point is truly recondite."

This verse refers to a Zen secret. I cite it here because this idea is quintessential in martial arts. People who do not study Zen will find it quite hard to comprehend.

In the context of martial arts, "myriad conditions" means all the actions of adversaries; the mind turns with each and every action. For example, when an opponent raises his sword, your mind turns to the sword. If he whirls to the right, your mind turns to the right; if he whirls to the left, your mind turns to the left. This is called "turning along with myriad situations."

"The turning point is truly recondite." This is the eye of martial arts. When the mind does not leave any traces in any particular place, but turns to what lies ahead, with the past dying out like the wake of a boat, not lingering at all, this should be understood as the turning point being truly recondite.

To be recondite is to be subtle and imperceptible; this means the mind not lingering on any particular point. If your mind stops and stays somewhere, you will be defeated in martial arts. If you linger where you turn, you will be crushed.

Since the mind has no form or shape, it is basically invisible; but when it clings and lingers, the mind is visible as such in that condition. It is like raw silk: dye it red and it becomes red, dye it violet and it becomes violet. The human mind also manifests visibly when it is attracted and fixated by things. If you are attracted to boys, eventually people will notice. When the thought is within, the impression appears outwardly.

When you are watching an opponent's moves carefully, if you let your mind linger there, you will lose at martial arts. The verse cited above is quoted to illustrate this point. I omit the last two lines of the verse. For Zen study, it is necessary to know the whole verse; in martial arts, the first two are enough.

MARTIAL ARTS AND BUDDHISM

There are many things in martial arts that accord with Buddhism and correspond to Zen. In particular, there is repudiation of attachment and avoidance of lingering on anything. This is the most urgent point. Not lingering is considered quintessential.

A courtesan wrote this poem in response to one by the Buddhist priest Saigyō:

If you ask as a leaver of home,
I simply think you should
not let your mind linger
on a temporary dwelling

In martial arts we should deeply savor the last lines, and see if we are not like this. No matter what kind of secret transmission you obtain and what move you employ, if your mind lingers on that move, you will have lost in martial arts. It is essential to practice an attitude of not dwelling on anything, be it the actions of an opponent, your own skills, or slashing and stabbing.

YES AND NO

Master Longji said to a group, "The pillar of affirmation does not see the pillar. The pillar of denial does not see the pillar. Having gotten rid of affirmation and denial altogether, attain understanding within affirmation and denial."

This story is to be applied to all arts. A certain teacher told it to me, and I thought of its application to martial arts, so I record it here.

As for the pillar of affirmation and the pillar of denial, this means that judgments of right and wrong, good and bad, stand firmly in the heart, affirmation and denial being like pillars standing. Insofar as keeping in mind something that is right will become onerous all of a sudden, it will be even more onerous if it is something wrong. Therefore the saying has it that you do not see the pillar. This means that you should not look at the pillars of affirmation and denial, right and wrong.

These judgments of good and bad are sicknesses of the mind. As long as these sicknesses do not leave the mind, whatever you do is not good. Therefore the saying goes that we should attain understanding within affirmation and denial after having gotten rid of affirmation and denial. This means that after having detached from affirmation and denial, you should then mix in with affirmation and denial, rising from the midst of affirmation and denial to the supreme state.

The eye detached from affirmation and denial is truly hard to attain, even if you have understood Buddhism.

Truth and Untruth

"Even truth is to be relinquished, to say nothing of untruth." In this passage, "truth" means really true teaching. Even really true teaching should not be kept in the mind once you have become completely enlightened. Thus "even truth is to be relinquished."

After you have realized true teaching, if you keep it in your chest, it pollutes your heart; how much more so does untruth! Since even truth is to be relinquished, to say nothing of untruth, this should not be kept in your heart. That is what this passage says.

Having seen all true principles, do not keep any of them in your chest. Let go of them cleanly, making your heart empty and open, and do what you do in an ordinary and unconcerned state of mind. You can hardly be called a maestro of martial arts unless you reach this stage.

I speak of martial arts because military science is my family business, but this principle is not limited to martial arts; all arts and sciences, and all walks of life, are like this. When you employ martial arts, unless you get rid of the idea of martial arts, it is a sickness. When you shoot, unless you get rid of the idea of shooting, it is a sickness of archery.

If you just duel and shoot with a normal mind, you should have no trouble with the bow and you should be able to wield the sword freely. The normal mind, not upset by anything, is good for everything. If you lose the normal mind, your voice will quiver whatever you try to say. If you lose the normal mind, your hand will quiver if you try to write something in front of others.

The normal mind keeps nothing in the heart, but lightly relinquishes the past, so that the heart is empty and therefore is the normal mind. People who read Confucian books, failing to understand this principle of emptying the mind, only concern themselves with "seriousness." Seriousness is not the ultimate realization; it is training in the first couple of steps.

NOTES

p. 97   *Weapons are instruments of ill omen*. This is a paraphrase of the Taoist classic *Tao Te Ching*, chapter 31. Yagyū's opening remarks follow Taoist theories; see *The Book of Leadership and Strategy* and *Wen-tzu*, listed in the Bibliography.

p. 101   A strategy to give life to many people by killing the evil of one person. Most wars do the opposite, sacrificing many people for the sake of a few. Buddhist theory on killing as an act of mercy is found in the great Mahāparinirvāna-sūtra, elucidated by the Tiantai master Huisi in these terms: "If enlightening beings practice mundane tolerance and thus do not stop evil people, allowing them to increase in evil and destroy true teaching, then these enlightening beings are actually devils, not enlightening beings."

p. 102   *The Great Learning*. This is an ancient Chinese treatise (*Da Xue*, Japanese *Daigaku*), one of the Four Books of Neo-Confucianism, on which orthodox education in Japan under martial rule was founded. The Four Books are the *Analects* of Confucius, the works of Mencius, *Balance in the Center*, and *The Great Learning*. *The Great Learning* is the easiest of these books and generally was the first to be memorized and studied in primary school.

p. 104 *Entering from learning into no learning*. In Buddhist terms, "no learning" represents the state of a graduate of the phase of self-liberation, who has nothing more to learn for personal salvation.

p. 104 *Mood and will*. "Mood" here should be understood in a wider than usual sense, to embrace the whole range of meaning of state of mind and disposition of psychic energy. The original term (*ki*) is untranslatable in itself, assuming as it does many meanings and nuances according to usage, especially in compound terms. In the context of martial arts, it should be noted that the Japanese word *ki* does not in fact coincide in meaning with the Chinese word *qi*, in spite of the facts that they are originally the same word and some of the psychological aspects of the handling of *ki*/*qi* are indeed similar.

p. 105 *Appearance and intention*. See *The Japanese Art of War* for further discussion of these terms.

p. 109 *The sandalwood state of mind*. This refers to striking twice at once with the same alignment.

p. 121 *The normal mind.* This does not refer to conventional normalcy, which is nothing but conformity to inculcated expectations, but normalcy in the Zen sense, which is the mind in its pristine state, not warped by environmental influences.

p. 124 *Like a wooden man.* Layman Pang was a famous lay Buddhist of eighth-century China. He studied with the greatest Chan masters of the time and was himself highly regarded as an adept. His wife, daughter, and son were also enlightened Chan Buddhists.

p. 125 *The free mind.* Master Zhongfeng Mingben was one of the distinguished Chan Buddhist masters of thirteenth-century China.

p. 127 *Three mysteries.* A Shingon Buddhist term referring to the actions of body, speech, and mind.

p. 129 *The rhythm of existence and nonexistence.* See *Tao Te Ching*, chapter 1.

p. 132 *The quiescent sword.* This refers to a state of potential, the hidden or dormant resources or possibilities of an individual, group, or situation.

p. 149 *Original countenance.* A Zen term for the pristine mind untrammeled by acquired habits of thought.

p. 149 *The energy of the blood.* Rendered literally here for the purposes of Yagyū's argument, *kekki* refers to so-called animal spirits or hot blood, vigor, ardor, vehemence, impetuosity, animal courage, blind daring, etc.

p. 153 The "No Sword" scroll goes to an even higher level. The art of "swordlessness" is the way to achieve security even when unarmed, how to accomplish tasks even when you have no resources.

p. 159 *Saint Manora* is reckoned as the twenty-second patriarch of Zen Buddhism in India. The last two lines of the verse cited run, "When you recognize nature and accord with its flow, there is no more elation, and no more sorrow." The great Japanese psychiatrist Morita Masatake often quoted this verse. Yagyū's deliberate omission of the last lines demonstrates the lack of complete coincidence between Zen and martial arts.

p. 161 *Saigyō* was a very famous Japanese poet of the twelfth century. Born in 1118, Saigyō was originally a soldier but abandoned the world at the age of twenty-three to become a Buddhist priest. He spent much of his life traveling and passed away in 1190. The poem cited by Yagyū is part of an extremely well-known incident in the travels of the great poet-monk, which took place one evening when he sought lodging for the night. One of the morals of the story, aside from the obvious message about impermanence and nonattachment, is that a courtesan may understand Buddhism as well as or better than a distinguished priest. Being able to see objectively without dwelling on preconceived expectations is also an art of war.

p. 161 Longji was a distinguished Chinese Chan (Zen) master of the Xuansha school in the late classical era of Chan. He lived from 869 to 928.

p. 163 *Truth and untruth.* The passage cited illustrates one of the hallmarks of Mahayana Buddhism. It is from a very popular scripture known in Japanese as the *Kongo-kyō,* or *Diamond Sutra.* This scripture was a favorite of lay people in China and of Zen Buddhists in Japan, where it was ritually recited as part of a common Zen liturgy.

BIBLIOGRAPHY

As Miyamoto Musashi emphasizes in his guidelines for students, martial artists in the Japanese warrior traditions were admonished to develop rounded mentalities and broad perceptions by studying cultural arts along with military science. The following books represent essential elements of East Asian martial and cultural traditions.

The Art of War. Translated by Thomas Cleary. Boston: Shambhala Publications, 1988. The most eminent Chinese classic of strategy, also studied by Japanese warriors.

The Book of Leadership and Strategy. Translated and edited by Thomas Cleary. Boston: Shambhala Publications, 1992. This book is a compendium of classical Taoist teachings, spiritual and cultural as well as political and martial. Yagyū Munenori's Zen teacher Takuan was also a student of Taoism, which is generally considered to have been an ancient congener of Zen Buddhism.

The Essential Confucius. Translated and presented by
Thomas Cleary. San Francisco: Harper San Francisco, 1992. The sayings of Confucius were regularly
memorized in Japanese primary schools for centuries. Acquaintance with Confucius is absolutely in-
dispensable for understanding the traditional fabric
of East Asian societies.

The Japanese Art of War, by Thomas Cleary. Boston:
Shambhala Publications, 1991. An analysis of the
influences of martial rule on Japanese culture, including a discussion of the relationship between the
ways of the warriors and Zen Buddhism.

Mastering the Art of War. Translated and edited by
Thomas Cleary. Boston: Shambhala Publications,
1989. Illustrative elucidations of the principles of
the classic Art of War, including moral and social
teachings paralleling the work of Yagyū Munenori,
and war stories demonstrating tactics paralleling
the work of Miyamoto Musashi.

Wen-tzu. Translated by Thomas Cleary. Boston:
Shambhala Publications, 1991. Attributed to Lao-
tzu, the Wen-tzu is one of the great classics of ancient Taoism, presenting teachings on the arts of
strategy within the broader social and psychological context.

Zen Essence. Translated and edited by Thomas Cleary.
Boston: Shambhala Publications, 1989. Fundamen-

tal Zen teachings and techniques presented by distinguished masters in easy conversational and discursive styles. The basic level of Zen mainly representedin this book is that primary freedom emphasized in martial arts by Yagyū Munenori.

Zen Lessons. Translated by Thomas Cleary. Boston: Shambhala Publications, 1989. Precious documents from distinguished Zen masters describing and illustrating the social and psychological aspects of Zen Buddhism, both genuine and imitative.

SHAMBHALA POCKET LIBRARY

The Dhammapada: A New Translation
of the Buddhist Classic
Translated and edited by Gil Fronsdal

Four Huts: Asian Writings on the Simple Life
Translated by Burton Watson

I Ching: The Book of Change
Translated by Thomas Cleary

The Integral Vision: A Very Short Introduction
Ken Wilber

Kabbalah: The Way of the Jewish Mystic
Perle Besserman

Lovingkindness:
The Revolutionary Art of Happiness
Sharon Salzberg

Meditations
J. Krishnamurti

Mindfulness on the Go
Jan Chozen Bays

The Path of Insight Meditation
Jack Kornfield and Joseph Goldstein

The Pocket Chögyam Trungpa
Compiled and edited by Carolyn Rose Gimian

The Pocket Dalai Lama
Edited by Mary Craig

The Pocket Meister Eckhart
Edited by David O'Neal

The Pocket Pema Chödrön
Edited by Eden Steinberg

The Pocket Rumi
Edited by Kabir Helminski

The Pocket Thich Nhat Hanh
Compiled and edited by Melvin McLeod

The Pocket Thomas Merton
Edited by Robert Inchausti

Siddhartha
Hermann Hesse; translated by Sherab Chödzin Kohn

Song of Myself
Walt Whitman; edited by Stephen Mitchell

The Spiritual Teaching of Ramana Maharshi
Ramana Maharshi

Tao Teh Ching
Lao Tzu; translated by John C. H. Wu

Walden: Selections from the American Classic
Henry David Thoreau

The Wisdom of the Buddha
Compiled and edited by Anne Bancroft

The Wisdom of Tibetan Buddhism
Edited by Reginald A. Ray